FOURTEEN DAYS

A Memoir of Love, Loss, and Quarantine Hell

Momoko Uno

Dedication

In loving memory of my mom

We have all lost so much. I hope you can look within your hearts and see that where there is loss, courage grows.

Acknowledgment

I would like to first and foremost thank Joselin Linder for her guidance in making lemonade out of lemons. She had a challenging task, as I only had half a moldy lemon to work with. Thank you for making possible what seemed impossible.

To Emily Sandack for making grammar fun! I may never remember when I should write out numbers or overcome my phobia of using commas, but at least I'm more aware of being grammatically inappropriate. I'm grateful for your patience and kindness.

To Gotham Writers Workshop and all their brilliant teachers. You helped me heal my English writing karma.

To Angelique de Wolf and Stephanie Jones for holding the light when my soul had fallen down a dark rabbit hole. They both reminded me there's more to human life than gnawing on baby carrots. Thank you for being angels.

A very special thank you to Janice Zwail, another angel and bearer of light, whose prayers saved me during quarantine.

Stephen Barnard for making sure I didn't lose my mind. Or provide me with a map when it was lost.

My sisters, Etsuko and Keiko, for holding our stories of our mother in our hearts and sharing the burden of our loss together.

To my soul family, you know who you are. In particular, Angela Ueckerman, Joseph Maggio, Scott Andersen, and Lily Tung. Thank you for decades of support and love.

To Ron and Mary Hulnick at the University of Santa Monica and all the students. Words are not enough. The three-foot toss really works! Love and Light to you all.

To all my colleagues and patients at Omni Wellness, who collectively create a place of kindness and healing. Thank you for the opportunity to learn from all of you. It has been an honor to be of service.

To all the dance studios and friends in New York City and Westchester. In particular, Central Park Dance for providing a nurturing place to grow as a dancer. To my belly dance teacher, Coco Ballantyne, who miraculously appeared when I returned from quarantine. An act of divine intervention. Jennifer Archibald and Eric Campros for their dedication to their art and commitment to teaching. You are both geniuses. To all my ballet teachers, in particular Kat Wildish, Tobin Eason, and Mr. G.

My deepest gratitude to Cynthia Williams and her team for their expertise, honesty and professionalism.

And thank YOU for reading my book. I hope my story brings you hope. You are not alone in your grief and pain. By sharing our stories, we can heal together. May you find the courage to open your hearts to love again.

When life throws you poop, use it as fertilizer to grow.

Table of Contents

ARRIVAL

About a month before the COVID-19 pandemic hit, I was riding the subway home in New York City. It was February 2020, we had all heard of the coronavirus, but most Americans were still in denial that the world was on the cusp of change. Typically, my rush hour commute home involved being compressed to half my volume in an overcrowded subway car—this day was no exception. It had been raining, so the floors were slippery and had that unmistakable, dirty subway, wet floor smell, which is a unique NYC transit stench that I haven't encountered anywhere else in the world.

I stood holding onto the horizontal pole, not only to stabilize myself, but to air out my armpits, overheating in my heavy winter coat. It was steamy; the windows fogged over with the overly zealous heating system and packed-together bodies adding to the overall grossness of the moment. I hovered over a potential empty seat—as opposed to an *actual* empty seat. The trick was to read the body language of the already-seated passengers. Most people about to get off the subway start to ready themselves by checking their belongings and glancing upward to prepare for their exit. Making eye contact with the seated person was key. Usually, a quick nod of acknowledgment was enough to ensure that the seat exchange was about to happen and the person standing next to me was out of the game. A dizzyingly quick left and right look to check for the pregnant, elderly, or disabled person, otherwise, you would discover quickly that a fraction of a second of hesitation was a guaranteed forfeiture of a seat for your tired bum. Growing up in Australia, one of my favorite games to play at birthday parties was musical chairs. I never won because I was too distracted as a child, but I think following my NYC subway seat experience, I would fare better with this game now.

Once seated, I received disappointing and scary news. A text from my sisters in Australia arrived, telling me that my mother's kidney transplant, of which she had been the recipient from an altruistic donor over a decade ago, was being rejected. Teary-eyed for my mother's decline, I sat with my heavy commuting bag on my lap, listening to music on my phone. "Lovely Day" by Bill Withers was playing, and the woman sitting squished up next to me looked at the song, then looked up at my face and asked, "Are you having a lovely day?"

I responded truthfully, "I can't say it's all that lovely, actually."

"Do you need a hug?" she asked, her arms wide open. "You look like you could do with a big hug."

"Thanks, but I'm good," I lied. "I actually don't like hugs." I tried to sound sincere, as the woman sitting on the far side of the

Hugger and I exchanged wide eyes of silent laughter.

A year and a half later, the pandemic in full swing, I left my preteen children behind, their father living close by, and I flew out of JFK airport. My mother's prognosis had worsened overnight. I desperately wanted to see her, and had already had to cancel three trips to fly back to Perth, Australia, my childhood home, due to the increasingly impossible travel restrictions.

My mother and I had our run-of-the-mill type of mother-daughter issues. When I was six, I decided that I was a descendant of an alien race and my mother had adopted me. She argued that it was unlikely as she had been there to witness my birth. We agreed to disagree. Although the feeling eventually became a lesser point of contention, I still felt untethered deep into adulthood—that somehow I didn't belong. My mom was religious. She was a Zen Buddhist. Although I respected her devotion to her religious path, it didn't capture my soul's attention, which caused an unspoken yet palpable disconnection between us, especially during my youth. Despite the difference in our philosophical approaches to life, my mother was always very supportive of my major life choices. I once asked her what I should be when I grew up and she answered, "You need to figure out what makes you happy."

That quest for happiness took me all over the world. While I wish I could say something corny like, "And then I discovered happiness was in my heart all along," that wasn't true at all. But I know I would have been unhappy if I had stayed in Perth. I needed to find my way to the Big Apple, where I found my acquired family. En route, however, there were long periods of feeling like a dissociated body, free falling through space, living without a base and not knowing where to call home. I adopted the theory that home is where the house is, but that left me without either grounding or roots. Maybe there was a deeper spiritual message pertaining to feeling like an alien adoptee, after all. At least this sense of disconnection from my family made it easier for me to leave my hometown without much thought.

The pivotal point in my relationship with my mother occurred when I became a mother for the first time. She came to Brooklyn for six weeks and did everything from grocery shopping to cooking to laundry. She cleaned, walked the dogs, and made fun of my beached-whale appearance.

My midwife rechristened my forty-hour labor "a triumphant birth," although there were moments I thought I touched death—or at least I wanted to die. For the first time in my life, I let my mother take care of me, and all those differences we had experienced no longer mattered. I remembered how much she loved me and experienced immense gratitude for having her in my life. At the same time, I too, became a mother, feeling unconditional love for my child. As my mother's health became more fragile, it became

4

more important for me to see her often, whether in Perth, Japan, or on a destination vacation.

As her life was coming to an end, I knew I wanted to see my mother; to take care of her like she had taken care of me; to show her that I cared about her, even if that meant just being present. I was aware that she understood my feelings and knew I cared, but I needed to express my care for her, to offer comfort in any way possible.

As a medical practitioner working at times with very ill patients over the last two decades, I learned the value of just being present, listening, and helping them to be comfortable when there was nothing left I could actually do from a medical perspective. Even if a cure may not be available, healing can still take place. There wasn't anything specific that I needed to heal for my mother, but I wanted to be in her presence again, to experience her spirit, to hold her hand, and to have her jokingly remind me that her skin was still softer and better than mine.

Up to the last time I saw my mother, she still held my hand when we crossed the road. It was so sweet and one of those things, I decided to continue to do with my growing children, even if just to embarrass them.

Despite this deep desire to be with my mother and to connect with her one last time, I had hesitated to go to Perth sooner because the thought of being stuck in hotel quarantine was overwhelming. The stories of the emotional agony of isolation and confinement, pushing people's mental health to the edge of insanity, was an experience I felt I could forego. The whole world had been experiencing isolation due to the pandemic, and though I had been living with my children, I recognized the social deficit that had taken place in the last year. So, adding on top of that, an even more concentrated form of isolation, was less appealing than a root canal without anesthesia.

Life is hard enough without intentionally seeking out torturous situations. Much like mentally tossing around the pros and cons of going on a date with a really, really hot serial killer, dating Ted Bundy—no matter how lonely I may be or how charming he is—isn't going to end well. This was one of those situations I feared would end poorly.

Simultaneously, I battled a fear of looking uncaring to my family or friends if I didn't travel to see my mother. Concern that my lack of willingness to travel and endure quarantine would be seen as a character flaw might have been, admittedly, the greatest motivating factor to go. When asked by one of my coworkers when I was going to visit my mom, could I really look at them and reply, "I'm not gonna bother. I'll watch her die on Zoom from the comfort of my couch. That's good enough for me." As an adult, this clear lack of personal integrity and need for external validation was an enlightening, albeit unwanted, revelation. Yet even this self-awareness was not enough to deter me from getting on the plane.

I remained conflicted about traveling up to the last second and thought about not going even as I boarded the flight. As the doors closed, I passively committed. It was 10:30 p.m. on April 22, 2021. I wanted to get through it as quickly and painlessly as possible. I yearned to see my mother, but the polarizing fears of traveling during a pandemic, getting on the longest flight on the planet, and dealing with all the logistics of being away for many weeks, was a huge dilemma. I sat on the plane, wondering if I had made a wise choice.

It was too late now to turn around. I looked around the plane to see what other suckers had joined my pathetic club of spineless humans who just needed to look good to others and realized I was one of only four passengers on my flight from New York City to Singapore: two in economy and two in business class. I had been forced to upgrade to business class when the airline informed me there were no economy tickets left.

Simple mathematics would conclude that there were at least two hundred seats still available, or I should clarify, two hundred *empty* seats, none of which were actually available. I'm not sure what happened there with that miscommunication, as I doubted that social distancing needed to be that extreme on any flight. Weeks after I returned to the U.S., I contacted the airline to complain about my forced $5,000 upgrade. They tried to convince me that within twelve hours of buying my ticket, everyone else had canceled due to Australia's travel restrictions. Each state in Australia had a different cap on the number of international travelers allowed into the state every week. The cap went up and down depending on the amount of COVID cases that had entered the specific state. There were also prolonged periods when some states closed their borders completely for weeks at a time until the coronavirus cases were at a manageable level. Therefore, the airline's reasoning could have been plausible if Western Australia had reduced its cap on international travelers. But during these twelve hours, Western Australia did *not* reduce their cap for incoming travelers, so it's highly improbable that this was the case. It would have been more believable if the airline had told me that all two hundred people had actually gotten food poisoning simultaneously and were tied to their toilets. In the end, no money or time was returned to me and I gave up the fight.

From New York, we connected in Singapore, then flew to Perth, my final destination and hometown. All the passengers to Perth were placed on four buses to check into the same hotel. It took about two and a half hours from landing to check-in—far less than what I had expected, having heard horror stories of others clocking more than eight hours with no access to food or water. Maybe my quarantine wasn't going to be so bad after all!

We carried our bags ourselves from the airport onto the bus. The walk took more than ten minutes, as we were instructed to walk in a single file while maintaining social distance. If anyone stopped, we all stopped.

The entrance to the hotel seemed rather strange for what was advertised as five-star. I swiveled my head around to get a panoramic view. The lobby looked more like a trendy underground bar— probably because it was. We had entered the hotel through a back way, complete with a long bar top, and the ambiance of an assassination line. It was actually a makeshift entrance that was created for the "red zone." The hotel we were staying in was divided between "regular" guests and the ones who might have cooties. The red zone guests checked in through the discreet back-alley entrance to ensure the regular and cootie guests never crossed paths. The general manager referred to us as his "special guests" with "special status." Some of the major hotels had contracts with the government to quarantine international travelers, as the hotel industry struggled to stay afloat with the plummeting number of tourists. Although risky for the hotel staff, getting a contract like this was their only means of keeping their doors open for business.

A plexiglass partition hovered above the counter, behind which stood two hotel staff checking in guests. We referred to ourselves as inmates, as we soberly awaited our turn to hand ourselves over to the two-week-long hotel quarantine mandated by the Australian government for all international travelers. New Zealand was the only exception, having entered into a travel bubble with Australia.

The plexiglass, about two-by-three feet, was suspended slightly lopsidedly from the ceiling, clearing a foot above the countertop. I theorized that air must not flow in Australia, the plexiglass commanding the air molecules not to flow around it. Otherwise, why bother with this barrier at all? It offered as much coverage as crotchless panties.

Eight staff members stood pinned against the interior walls of the lobby anywhere from six feet to twenty feet away, pointing fingers and shouting various instructions to everyone coming off the bus from Perth International Airport. I have found that most people are naturally kind and when given the opportunity, do want to help. But this was a *hands off, you're on your own* commando-style check-in. "You next! Stop! Back! No touch!"

All the hotel staff were in need of unsolicited hugs, I decided, suddenly channeling the Hugger from the subway all those months ago. I'd risk being arrested for breaking the 1.5-meter social distancing rule to hug someone. Interestingly, Australian social distancing is about 1.5 feet shy of the 6-foot requirement in the U.S.

Maybe in Australia people don't sneeze as strongly as Americans do, so less social distancing is required. Americans, after all, do everything bigger than anyone else. Having just transited through Singapore, I learned they only sneeze three feet over there. I could fully outstretch my arms three feet and give everyone a Singaporean (being Asian, I could easily pass as Singaporean), social-distance-abiding hug tap on their shoulders. "There, there. All better!"

The arrival at the hotel wasn't a typical welcome with a rush of porters to help me with my luggage, but rather an ear-piercing "STEP BACK BEHIND THE YELLOW LINE!" I looked down and noticed my toe hadn't crossed, but had, in fact, covered it. "Come on man, seriously?" said my inside voice, as I daringly imagined myself overstepping the line by a whole foot, hands on my hips and giving him my best teenage-rebellious look of *What are you gonna do, dude?* But instead, I wiggled my foot back behind the line, shrank a few inches and muttered, "Sorry," as I watched the woman in front of me struggle with her bags. I called out to her, "You need help?"

The same guard yelled, "Don't touch her!"

His passionate voice made me want to warmly embrace him. "Aww, who's having a bad day and needs a hug? You!"

There were police everywhere to undoubtedly control any potential fugitives. I looked around curiously to see if I had the opportunity to get out before the quarantine happened. I wasn't too surprised to hear there were quite a few who attempted to make a run for it. Could I? I quickly assessed the situation at hand and planned out my 100 percent foolproof escape plan. I ran through some options and decided my best bet would have been to dress up as a recycling trash can. I obviously couldn't get off the plane that way, so I'd need to make a quick change in the bathroom while in the arrival hall. I'd position myself innocently outside the bathroom, cautiously peering out to see if the coast was clear to move a few feet whenever possible. It could take days, but it would be worth it when I finally made it out of the exit. The only issue was that I didn't have a costume. Right? That was the *only* issue? My options were to be a law-abiding citizen and surrender to the hotel quarantine for two weeks, or spend six years in jail.

Given the twelve-hour time difference—it was about 4 a.m. back home—I walked into the hotel in a semi-lucid, dreamlike stupor. I was hungover without any alcohol. In addition, having left my home almost thirty-six hours prior to arrival at the hotel, jet lag was setting in quickly. It was like I had stepped into a funhouse, and everything looked distorted.

Standing with my two suitcases, one in each hand, and my messenger bag on my shoulder, I watched a frail woman in line struggling with her luggage down the narrow, flimsy, plywood ramp which barely held her weight as she entered. The plywood looked like it had been used beyond its retirement as it buckled under her petite frame. She had one of those unruly suitcases—every wheel had its own agenda. I watched her pancake flat onto the top of her suitcase as she held up her ID to the check-in staff.

I had read that most hotels were all equally atrocious and the only hotel that had decent food was the Mercure, which had just closed down the previous day due to two positive COVID cases that guests contracted after staying in the hotel. Authorities blamed the ventilation system as the cause of transmission of the virus. They had been running the hotel under quarantine for almost a year at this point, with other positive COVID cases, and all of a sudden, the vents were the cause of cross-contamination in the hotels, which seemed a bit odd. People argued it was a political move to reduce the cap of people coming through quarantine, as the majority of Australians wanted to shut down the borders completely and not allow anyone in or out of the country.

Most coronavirus cases had been contracted by the hotel guards who patrolled the hallways. There was at least one account where a guard redefined his personal definition of patrolling to mean he should patrol *inside* a guest's room. He didn't just stop at patrolling inside the guest's room—he patrolled inside her vagina. If she didn't have COVID, he might have gotten away with his little patrolling escapade, but luck wasn't in his favor, as he too, got infected, and carried it out into the community.

The rules for quarantine state guests can only open the door with a mask on to quickly pick up a delivery and then immediately close the door. How did that jump from patrolling the hallways with a few seconds of eye contact between a guard and guest to masks off, pants down? Did their eyes meet during one lunch delivery as she reached out for her meat pie and found herself desiring more? Not just for fresh vegetables, which were also lacking and causing nutritional imbalances, but also to satisfy her carnal needs? In my end-of-quarantine review, I suggested that the hotel should offer generous carrot sticks with every meal—that could have taken care of both dietary and sexual needs.

As soon as I'd heard that we were staying at the Pan Pacific at the airport, I immediately joined an uncensored Facebook group for Pan Pacific Perth. I also joined the official group, which was censored, and anything negative posted was immediately removed. I posted in the uncensored group, "Heading into PPP now, feeling a bit nervous."

People responded within minutes, "You have good reason to feel that way," "Good luck in hell," "The rooms are unhygienic," and "The food is inedible!" There was not one good post about the hotel, which was probably the sole purpose of an uncensored group. It was a place to vent about horrific experiences. Reading about the walls collapsing from flooding, moldy green bathrooms, and bug infestations, to mention a few atrocities that guests had experienced, sent shivers up my neck. The truth, I imagined, lay somewhere between the picture-perfect service that was portrayed in the censored group and the nightmare of the uncensored. Only time would tell where my personal experience would land on the spectrum.

In the uncensored group, it was previously posted that rooms higher up had been renovated, but the lower rooms were filthy. As it was a contactless stay, which meant no cleaning service, getting one of the nasty rooms was adding filth to an already challenging situation. Two solid weeks in even the most spotless room wouldn't be easy, but the thought of my only company being roaches and dust bunnies had me praying for a good room assignment. "Please, God, a room on the twentieth floor or higher."

"Here's your key to room 2025," the hotel attendant said, standing behind the Swiss cheese barrier. I breathed a sigh of relief as I reached out for the keys to my two weeks in hell.

Before I left for hell, the hotel agent asked me if I had any food allergies, as the hotel could accommodate certain dietary requirements. I had already made a plan for this. My sister would be bringing me supplies, and I wouldn't be eating their food. "I have life-threatening food allergies," I explained, "so I'd prefer to prepare my own food."

"We offer gluten-free meals," she said with an air of *I've heard this overly exaggerated story before.*

"It's not just gluten, I can't eat many things." Feeling dismissed was my default setting when talking about my food issues.

"The kitchen will be able to cater to any food allergies." She looked at me with a motionless face.

"I don't think it's safe for me to eat any prepared food." My resting bitch face behind a mask in full action.

"The chef will call you to discuss this matter further." She minimally raised one eyebrow.

"Can I decline the food?" I folded my arms.

"Ok, in that case, the kitchen will be sending you regular meals, and it's your choice to eat it or not."

I pursed my lips and furrowed my brow at the logic, but unfortunately, this is a discussion I'd had before. Having a medical degree specializing in integrative internal medicine, it often feels like a blow to my ego to get dismissed as being a wuss or making vague lifestyle choices, like having self-diagnosed food problems based on reading some fashion magazines. The fact is, a piece of fish will take me down, like ingesting a box of rat poison would any individual. I have potentially fatal reactions. Before I was diagnosed, I was often told it was all in my mind—an infuriating experience—and that my mind, not my body, was too weak to ingest nuts without turning bright red or to eat a small bite of fish without triggering a seizure that left me unconscious. I have a master's degree in psychology, and nowhere in my education did I read that my mind can overcome food allergies. Even knowing my educational background, most people just assumed I was crazy.

After years of my silent struggle with allergies, I was finally given the right diagnosis of mast cell activation syndrome (MCAS) as the medical community came up with a name for my haywire symptoms. There are safe foods, and then there are foods that are sometimes safe. The why remains scientifically elusive. It's funny that now that I actually have a name for all my symptoms, everyone says, "Oh wow, I'm sorry, that sounds totally legit." But without a name, the reaction was, "You're insane." I've found that my patients with unnamed illnesses, even those who appeared quite ill, similarly felt shame around some "mystery" illness that friends, family, and strangers insisted they had intentionally manufactured.

At the Pan Pacific Perth, only one person was permitted in the elevator at a time, and no one was allowed to touch anything. My floor was already pre-selected by the time I entered. I stood clutching my hands against my chest so I wouldn't accidentally contaminate anything, but my inner demon wanted to lick all the clean buttons. Having had two COVID tests in the past week, the likelihood of being positive was slim, but maybe the guy I'd seen

17

coughing on the bus a few rows behind me was positive.

When I reached the twentieth floor, two guards pointed me toward my room. The same woman who had been in front of me at reception dragged her mammoth suitcase sideways on the carpeted hallway, dimly lit by red emergency floor lights as if we were in an eerie B-grade horror film. As she began to cry in frustration, I felt terrible for her. "They aren't very helpful, are they?" I asked, trying to offer her something since I could do nothing. "I'm sorry I can't help you."

"I'll be fine," she replied unconvincingly as tears soaked her mask.

I found my room—the place I would be spending the next few weeks of my life—and I took a deep breath. An intense sense of panic and claustrophobia engulfed me when I walked in. *Fourteen days. Oh my god, how am I going to do this? Breathe, breathe*, I told myself. *We can do this one day at a time.*

The room was clean enough, with a queen-size bed with crisp white sheets and a desk and chair, as well as a chaise lounge. The two windows were large and let in a generous amount of light. However, they were filthy on the outside—a pity since the view was marvelous looking out onto East Perth with slivers of the Swan River peering between the tall buildings across the street.

I unpacked my bags and settled in. I had packed just enough

clothes to rotate for a few days, knowing they offered laundry services so I wouldn't need two weeks' worth. As kitchen appliances were forbidden in hotels, I had to sneak them in. In fact, the bulk of the weight of my luggage included a portable induction stove top with a pot, a rice cooker, a food warmer, a water purifier, cooking oil, and a selection of herbal teas. I set up my mini kitchen and pantry for my stay. I opened up the mini fridge to add the two extra containers of food that I had bought—my backup food in case I was delayed in transit. The fridge was barely cold, but it was better than nothing, although I wondered if the temperature was even cold enough to store my food safely. "Probably not," I said out loud, a habit that would only increase as the days went by. I felt a shiver of anxiety at the prospect of eating spoiled food. With my food allergies and potential anaphylaxis, I didn't have much room for mistakes. It was too much to think about right then, so I stuffed the thought into a dark crevice in my subconscious, where it would certainly ferment and gas out at a future unexpected and inappropriate time—hopefully unlike my meals.

My sister Keiko, who lived locally with her daughter, husband, and adorable puppy that doubled as a floor mop, kindly dropped off my first box of groceries and some fragrant sprays. She'd heard it could get pretty stinky in those rooms. Keiko was born less than two years after I was. I had vague memories of being jealous of her when she came home from the hospital. I watched my mother burp her and asked if I could burp her too, which was an excuse to hit her instead. I got in big trouble, but I felt justified since she *had* taken my mother's attention away. When I was about four years old, I cut Keiko's hair every time I could run off with scissors. My mother didn't like that much either, but I thought the bald patches looked really cool. Keiko showed artistic and creative potential from a very young age and, without any training, could arrange flowers beautifully. After I was told I had no flower arrangement skills at age ten, I asked eight-year-old Keiko how she assembled flowers, and she responded, "I feel it and create what looks good in my mind." I had no idea what she was talking about. Come to think of it, I still don't.

Keiko joined our mother in the jewelry industry and then branched out with a successful solo career after our mother retired. My second sister Etsuko was born when I was five. I remember more clearly meeting her at the hospital than Keiko. Etsuko was born a month early, but she was already trying to lift her head out of the crib the day after she was born. My father said, "She's going to be a precocious child," and she was.

My favorite memory of Etsuko as an infant was seeing her take naps on my mom's belly while lying back on the chaise lounge in the living room. She finished high school when she was sixteen, and after going to graduate school at Rockefeller University in New York City, she decided to pursue a career as a computer animation artist. She then returned to Australia, but during her stay in New York, we met up every weekend to take drawing classes together, a practice that became her impetus to change careers. Etsuko also became successful in her career as a biomedical animator.

I spritzed the room with fragrant sprays. I had turned off the A/C as I had become paranoid about the ventilation systems carrying the coronavirus as the news had portrayed. My room was stuffy, and although it passed as clean, the air felt heavy, like I was in an unventilated locker room that had just been vacated by a class of teenage boys. My sinuses felt like I had inhaled a sludgy mix of Speed Stick, sweat, and unwashed pit hair. I felt a little sick, probably a mix of anxiety, fatigue, and my own horrific body odor from not having showered in two days. I had proved wrong the theory that Asians don't smell bad.

For the first time in maybe weeks, I had a moment to slow down. Slowing down isn't something I have done well with in my life. I've excelled at zooming through life at an ungodly speed. I might have been able to accomplish more things, but more is just more, it's definitely not better, and I think I've missed out on the finer details and delicate nuances of life as a result. One of the most memorable pieces of feedback I have ever received was that I do everything very quickly, which includes making mistakes. When I make a mistake, it's usually a royal one because I'm already so far down the path of errors compared to the average person. I construct quickly, and I deconstruct even faster. When it comes to any anxious thoughts, I can whip them up and either allow them to explode into being or let them settle and lie dormant, waiting to take life with a single stoked ember. All the anticipatory anxiety I had experienced before traveling, I had been too busy to rationally process during my journey. It had now begun to flood my thoughts. I started to think about all the ways I could potentially die while I was in quarantine, and while I was at it, all the ways I could kill myself too. There was an abundance of ways to go, including abductions, military air raids, avalanches, etc. I began to kill myself off in dozens of creatively constructed ways. This self-induced anxiety bordering on panic made my heart race, and soon I was afraid of giving myself a heart attack. I ran the risk of putting myself out of commission before I ended my first few hours in quarantine, so I forced myself to lay down on the chaise lounge and put my hands on my belly. Deep breaths into my tummy on the count of five and exhaled to six as I repeated, "It's gonna be OK, we got this, it's gonna be OK…." After all, we can only die once.

DAY ONE

Day one? Wasn't that yesterday? Nope, that was day zero. It might have been easier to call it a fifteen-day quarantine as everyone was so confused by this "day zero" start. I started quarantine at around 4 p.m. on April 24, 2021; however, the time that I would be released would be *exactly* two weeks from the time my flight landed in Perth, which was 2:16 p.m. So, on Saturday, May 8th, at 2:16 p.m., I would be allowed to step foot out of my cell. Fortunately, this was a reasonable time. There were others who landed at 2 a.m., which meant they could check out at 2 a.m. Since no one wanted to stay in quarantine any longer than they had to, I imagine many left in the middle of the night. But the health department did give exemptions for people willing to wait until the sun came up to check out, for example, if they had young children. But, like with everything else in this experience, there had to be written approval given ahead of time, and if you missed your window to file for an exemption, then you would be getting thrown out at 2 a.m. No exceptions! You did have the option of staying in another room in the "green zone" of the hotel after your official check-out time, but you would still need to officially check out and re-check in—rooms subject to availability. This meant you could end up waiting half a day for a room which would defeat the purpose of trying to avoid the middle-of-the-night eviction.

Waking up on my first official day was met with my body still on eastern standard time, and my mind split between realities: excitement to see my mother and the fear that I might not see her alive. I stumbled out of bed and looked outside. I had to pause for a second, step back, and look again. A stormtrooper was standing on a balcony in the apartment complex across the street. *I must still be dreaming or having hallucinations.* I thought while contemplating calling the mental health hotline. I took a picture of the stormtrooper and sent it to a few friends at home, asking if I was suffering from psychosis. I received affirmative responses that there was indeed a stormtrooper stationed there.

In the days to follow, many guests posted pictures of the stormtrooper on the hotel's Facebook group, and the hotel management confirmed nobody was insane—yet. Already, on the first day sitting in my comfortable cell, I was questioning my mental health.

A litany of thoughts chased through my mind: *I can't wait to see mom. I should have come a week earlier. It's only 8 a.m., and I feel like I need a nap.*

I fought the exhaustion and created a schedule for my days to come thinking the structure would be helpful to get through my experience. I knew that forcing my way through jet lag the first few days was the best way to acclimate to a new time zone. I sat down at the desk and pulled out the pad and pencil the hotel provided. The room felt smaller than yesterday. My mind must have been playing tricks on me.

According to one personality test, I was considered to lean 75 percent toward the extroverted spectrum. I thrived on human interactions and never needed much time alone to recharge. During the early days of the pandemic, sequestered away in my suburban house, I witnessed myself go into an emotional slump from the social withdrawal. Fortunately, I lived with my children and babysitter, so I had company. I can't imagine how much worse my social isolation experience would have been had I lived alone.

But I felt like I was missing something very important in my life like there was a new void, a loneliness and longing to connect that I only remembered experiencing when I was seventeen and moved abroad for the first time to Shanghai to pursue a medical degree. My first landing point was Fudan University, an undergraduate degree to ensure I had learned enough Chinese to go to medical school. I didn't know anyone, I couldn't speak any Chinese, and this was a time before cell phones, so most communication was done via letter writing. For an entire month, I didn't meet anyone. I figured I'd have to live in this state of isolation for the next decade or so, a fear thankfully truncated as I made friends from all over the world and had the best possible undergrad experience imaginable. That initial state of solitude was memorable and stood as a benchmark for isolation and loneliness.

The long-term effects of social isolation and loneliness have been known to significantly increase the likelihood of reducing one's overall health and to be a cause of premature death. Most of us experienced a version of this during the pandemic. According to one study, about two-thirds of the U.S. population have experienced pandemic-related isolation with increased anxiety.

The first morning of my quarantine, I woke up to a more concentrated form of isolation than ever before—at least my past experiences had permitted me to go outside. Some recent studies have suggested that about one in four people who have endured hotel quarantine in Australia will have long-term complications like post-traumatic stress disorder. PTSD happens when the brain is flooded into a state of panic and cannot reset back to a state of peace while reliving the initial trauma. It can feel like living in your worst nightmare every day and never waking up. Things that once had a neutral or positive meaning might now trigger anxiety and fear. According to one study, about 70 percent of travelers who went through hotel quarantine experienced some form of mental illness and were five times more likely to end up in an ER for mental health-related issues. With a post-graduate degree in psychology, I understood the problematic nature of the significant mental imbalance that occurs when perceived reality differs greatly from the objective.

Going into the experience with these statistics in mind felt scary. I wanted to avoid the chance of ending up in the ER by mistaking anxiety for a heart attack or even for reporting I was being attacked by a clan of vicious pixies trying to force-feed me a beer while watching an early rerun of an '80s sitcom. I recognized that I would need to stay as calm as possible to minimize any damaging effects on my brain and nervous system. It wasn't going to be easy. I was already entering into quarantine, not in the most stellar health, thanks to my allergies and my mother's state of unwellness. All of the stress and rushing home had started my stay in a deficit. It was like starting a marathon with a sprained ankle. I knew I was already in a compromised state.

Isolation felt like living in a box. Nobody could see me, and I couldn't see out. And as I retreated deeper into isolation, I was encapsulated by another box. Each box had a different label on it, like a façade that I showed the world. The outer box had a grimacing smiley emoji slapped on it; another box had an image of *The Scream* by Edvard Munch. With the passage of time, unable to connect with others, it was as if I contracted and became a smaller version of myself, retreating into additional boxes. Much like Russian nesting dolls, my innermost me felt encased in layer upon layer of invisible walls.

Shortly after my birth, my mother became critically ill and was hospitalized. English, not being her first language and being far away from her family, she was flown back to Japan for medical care. Around six months later, she arrived back in Perth, but according to stories, there were periods of "all hands on deck" for my mother's survival, and I had been unintentionally abandoned. I sometimes missed feedings and was left regularly—diaper unchanged. Getting childcare wasn't an easy task in a foreign language. Eventually, help arrived from Japan—extended family and hired nannies—but given the rotation of caregivers, those bonds were repeatedly broken. From this very early experience, I sometimes wonder if my default state of being became one of isolation.

Throughout my childhood, I frequently questioned if my mother even cared about me. Sometimes her behavior didn't indicate my needs were priorities. It was easy to make the assumption that I wasn't important to her. It was only much later, as an adult, that I managed to detach those experiences from my self-worth.

As an Asian living in Australia, with its predominantly white population, I felt even more isolated and, at times, even ostracized. Within my psyche lay this pre-existing condition of isolation inherent to my innermost self. Allowing myself to be vulnerable enough to trust people took time. I had friends. However, I developed a disproportionately independent operating system that perpetuated feelings of solitude and loneliness. In my psychology study, I learned how to heal and create a healthier dynamic of interdependence with others. My personal goal was that my relationships, whether business, friendships, family, or intimate, would have moments when each could be passive and active, giving and receiving. Everything that I had studied suggested that my innate hardwiring from repeated episodes of abandonment and neglect had cut me off from some important areas of self-awareness.

Babies who aren't soothed when crying will eventually stop crying. They simply stop asking for help. In many ways, my idea that I was an alien in a human body, trapped in a terrain that didn't make any sense and couldn't be mapped out, wasn't so far-fetched. Some studies have even shown that hunger, even for short periods during infancy, can lead to long-term depression for decades through adult life and increase the chances of suicide.

In my twenties, when I was getting my master's degree in psychology, the memory veil from my childhood started to recede. I discovered quite a bit about the hidden impulses behind my behaviors, both positive and negative. This by no means was easy, but with the help of the program—the healing power of a group all going through the same process and with the support of a skilled therapist—I was able to apply healing balm to my abandonment wounds. This process was not pretty. It was a particularly ugly phase in my life when I tapped into the repressed memories of being abandoned and neglected. I encountered the terror of not knowing if I would survive or ever see my parents again. The pain was excruciating, and a part of me thought I would die, while another part wanted to die because the experiences had been unbearable. Soul-crushing was a mild way to describe my journey into my shadow, and I got stuck in a deep depression as it took me about a year to unpack those blockages and rebuild myself in a healthy way. I saw where in my life I continued to isolate, abandon, and neglect myself, as this was what I primarily knew. At the end of a very dark phase of my life, I vowed to commit to happiness to the best of my ability and to take better care of myself.

During this challenging time, I was dating a guy, Adam, who was as sweet and charming as he was disorganized and chronically late. With his Doogie Howser meets Peter Pan persona, a fun, energetic, walking encyclopedia, he often kept me waiting for hours. He was not equipped to deal with my emotionally chaotic state. It was not his role to heal my trauma, and yet a part of me hoped he would. The more I valued the relationship, the greater the stakes became for losing it. His tardiness was a trigger for my anxiety about being abandoned.

About six months into our relationship, he broke up with me. After that, suicidal thoughts began to emerge. I refused medication, but if I were to do it over again, I hoped I'd take the antidepressants to make my life a lot easier, but that wasn't my path. Within a year, I had stabilized. And within two years, I was thriving. We got back together after a short separation and then stayed together for several years.

Severing a relationship is never easy, no matter the circumstances. After that relationship, I got better at breakups— binge-watching sappy sitcoms and consuming boxes of jelly donuts, with my friends feeding me lines like "It's his loss." I had close friendships that helped to keep me grounded. With them, I shared my innermost struggles and darkness. Our banter was easy and peppered with a rapid firing of jokes. It was a mix of both lightness and turning darkness into humor while being cognizant that the sun isn't supposed to shine everywhere. Some of those friendships I had fostered since I was in elementary school and others I had made as an adult, but I knew from a young age that the cornerstone for my mental well-being was largely dependent on the quality of those friendships.

I knew I could count on my close friends to be present for me. Decades ago, I had read in a self-help book that friendships were like a bank account: we can't just keep withdrawing from them, rather, we need to continuously make deposits, and with time and interest, the friendship account will grow. In times of need, we can make larger withdrawals. I tried to make sure that there was always a good balance in all my friendship accounts, as it was never a good feeling to be overdrawn. I also tried to reduce the friendships that

31

were more like a charity where there was little to no return.

I was born in the seventies when pregnant mothers still drank, and alcoholism was less demonized. My father, in particular, drank too much. Both my parents were in their mid-twenties, and their brains and identities were barely formed, subjecting all three of us to their dysfunctional relationship. Their divorce was the icing. Essentially, I believe I have always been on a trajectory of becoming a superb sociopath or, at best, pretty fucked up. Considering my less-than-ideal start to life, I'm surprised I even potty trained, let alone graduated from high school. In fact, when I told the school counselors and higher-education advisers I wanted to go to medical school, they unanimously recommended I go to a community college until I worked out a career more aligned with my aptitude.

Some of my earliest memories are of my mom being too ill to take care of me. I became her caretaker while sometimes denying my own needs. Young children are fundamentally egocentric, which means that before the age of seven, we tend to think that we are the cause of everything that happens to us. In my mind, my mother left me, not because she was sick and had to take care of herself, but because I had done something to cause her to leave me. This was the foundation of all my inner wiring at the deepest core of who I was. I was a little ant, fiercely equipped with full armor, ready to build a skyscraper on the sandy dunes of the Sahara Desert alone.

To reverse this pattern and recognize my needs took decades to accomplish. The goal obviously wasn't to become a charity case but rather for me to learn the important lesson that life is a give-and-take. And giving without receiving will eventuate in feelings of emptiness and anger, mistakes I know all too well, perpetuating the cycle of isolation.

Heading into quarantine, I was well aware of all my triggers. Even so, I went—even with the screaming neon sign lighting the phrase "Dumb choice." The fact that my mother was dying and would leave me was the opposing trigger, the one that made me go.

Regardless of all the self-improvement I had achieved over the last twenty-five years, I still had an unrelenting concern: Putting myself through quarantine, the potential death of my second parent, and being alone through this period of time without my typical support network or the structure, would inevitably push me over the edge and into the looney bin. But it was too late now. I was in quarantine, and there was no way out, or rather the only route out would be through a psych ward—a potentially worse outcome than just staying cooped up in quarantine. Sometimes in life, there are no good options, but there may be a pathway to pave that's not as bad. And at least from where I stood, the "less bad" journey seemed to be to stay put in quarantine rather than making a run for it or getting strapped into a straitjacket and thrown into a padded room.

*****

I joined a Facebook group called "Australians Stranded around the World." I had no idea that over a year after the pandemic had started, about forty thousand Australians were still stranded internationally and unable to make it back home. Some had been bumped off flights daily or weekly for an entire year. Many had given up and been given temporary residency where they were stranded, had opened up bank accounts, and had found jobs. I quickly discovered many parents had been separated from their children and some fathers hadn't even met their children who'd been born during the pandemic.

Australian citizens and permanent residents hadn't been able to return to take care of their sick family members due to low caps on incoming travelers. Every week, the cap that permitted people entering into every state changed depending on COVID cases in Australia, and there were times when the borders were completely closed for several weeks, leading to a huge backlog of people trying to funnel in. Many people didn't make it back on time before their family members passed away, and many more missed funerals. Australians able to get travel exemptions to enter and leave the country were few, thanks to the reality of low border permeability, preventing many from traveling. For many, the cost of flights became prohibitive or impossible as airlines were forced to raise their prices to account for these lowered caps or COVID restrictions for the maximum amount of people allowed on planes. Ticket prices often doubled or tripled, and the added financial hardship of being stranded overseas without a visa to work left thousands broke—not just monetarily speaking, but in spirit too.

Those lucky enough to be able to pay for a ticket were then forced through a government-controlled quarantine period at their first port of entry into Australia. It didn't matter if you were vaccinated or not, the process was the same for everyone. The quarantine facilities differed greatly from hotel to hotel and even more so from state to state. Western Australia (WA) had the most restrictive hotel quarantine, with windows that were bolted shut and without access to any outdoor space.

Everyone was mandated to quarantine in a hotel—there were absolutely no exemptions, even if you had a perfectly good empty apartment somewhere nearby. In WA, if you fell ill, you were transported to a hospital, unlike other states where there were "health hotels" for travelers who required additional medical attention, with doctors on site. Darwin had a facility dedicated to quarantine called Howard Springs, which offered single and family units with decks and kitchenettes. The guests were encouraged to sit outside on the deck and speak with their neighbors, which helped to maintain social contact and reduce some of the damaging effects of isolation and feelings of entrapment. They also had designated times for people to walk the grounds that included access to a pool. Pan Pacific also had a pool, which would have been a delight to use, but it was off-limits to us.

I've always loved chocolate; one of my little delights. One time when I was about ten, I couldn't rip open a chocolate wrapper, so I tried to eat it with the wrapper still on—without success. Any attempt to get a dip into the pool would have been futile, so occasionally, I longingly looked at the pool as if it were a giant piece of inaccessible chocolate—one I couldn't even chew with the wrapper on.

Sydney quarantine, unlike Perth, had apartments with full kitchens and washing machines for families. People with dietary concerns were accommodated with kitchens, and most other places had balconies and windows that opened too. Perth didn't offer any of these amenities. They only had single rooms and suites for families. Even people serving time in prison have time outdoors every day, but not in Perth quarantine. It was solitary confinement for fourteen days.

*****

I had packed some books, an iPad, and a yoga mat to occupy

myself. Friends had given me a list of things to watch on Netflix. I had no idea how to prepare for a hotel quarantine, as I had never done anything like it before. The airlines had a limit to what I could bring, too, so there wasn't enough space to bring a bouncy inflatable castle, StairMaster, or ballet barre. There was an option to rent a stationary bike, but it took up so much space in my small room, so I decided against it.

I took the advice of a fellow quarantine inmate to learn something new. I contemplated what I could possibly learn as I was pretty limited in terms of what one could do confined in a hotel room. What did I want to learn? Rock climbing wasn't feasible, although I'd be climbing the walls by the end of my stay. My mother introduced me to the love of dance when I was three. I quickly embraced her enthusiasm for all forms of dance, and I took ballet, tap, and jazz regularly. It was still one of my lingering regrets that I hadn't pursued it more seriously when I was younger, although I thoroughly immersed myself in dance as a hobby throughout my life. Many years ago, when my mother and I met up in Hawaii, we learned how to Hula together, and in Bali, we learned traditional Balinese dance. We had planned to take Nihon Buho, a traditional Japanese dance, the next time we traveled there. Dance was a passion that we shared, and given the fact that I was here to visit my mother, I decided I could learn a new form of dance. I wanted one that didn't require me to leap across the room and potentially injure myself. I couldn't do the polka as I didn't bring any invisible friends. I had no access to a pole either, so striptease was out, so I settled on belly dancing. It quickly turned into belly-up dancing, but at least I tried.

Mealtimes tended to vary by several hours; anyone struggling with low blood sugar would find it challenging. Sometimes lunch was at 10 a.m. or as late as 2 p.m., and dinner was at 4 p.m. or 8 p.m., as there was not enough staff to manage the distribution of meals and assist guest check-ins and outs, so they doubled up on many tasks.

There were at least three knocks on my door every day. The three semi-predictable ones were for meals. Then there were also knocks for deliveries and nurse visits. It was important to wait a minute after each knock to open the door to ensure that the hotel staff wasn't still in the hallway when you opened the door. I was required to use a new mask each time I opened the door and to put it on immediately beforehand. I was instructed to look through the peephole into the hallway to double-check that the staff was no longer visible before quickly grabbing what had been left for me. It was OK to open the door if a security guard was sitting outside your door but not the delivery staff. The security guards were hired by the health department, and the delivery staff worked for the hotel.

We were not permitted to leave our rooms under any

circumstances. There were cameras installed to cover every square foot of the hotel, and anyone seen leaving would be caught and penalized. During my stay, some inmates received calls from security and were told to stay in their rooms when, in fact, they had never even left. It didn't seem to be the most efficient system, and there were some false accusations. A friend of mine traveled back from Europe with her elderly father, who had been struggling with Alzheimer's. Every day, she told me, he tried to make a run for it into the hallways, sometimes naked. Young children who didn't like being confined in the hotel room were also common escapees.

Whenever I had to open the door, I would take an extra second to elongate my neck out to take a peek down the hallway in both directions. Sometimes the guards' seats were completely empty, and other times there were four guards sitting or standing around having a chit-chat. It seemed like there was no rhyme or reason as to when and how many guards were stationed in the hallways. If a guard was sitting opposite my room, I would often wave at him just to have some human contact. Sometimes I got a nod of acknowledgment. One time when I peeked out to pick up a grocery delivery, one of the guards had his mask down and was eating and drinking. Guards are only permitted to eat in the staff room, not within the international borders of hotel quarantine, where COVID transmissions were mostly speculated to occur. Nearly every time I saw a guard, they were sitting in their stations, noses in their phones, oblivious to what was going on. Australia was banking on keeping its country safe by a bunch of boys in their early twenties flipping through Instagram.

Once, a knock on my door came at a non-meal time. Excitedly, I forgot to look out the peephole before I opened it. A nurse and a guard were speaking with the inmate diagonally to my left. They quickly turned around as I opened the door, breaking quarantine instructions. "I'm so sorry. I forgot to look to see if anyone was out here." I stuttered nervously, afraid that the guard would arrest me on the spot for violating quarantine rules.

The nurse responded, "It's no problem to get that," and pointed to the vacuum cleaner I had requested. She was friendly, which took me by surprise as I had half expected to be executed on the spot. Regardless, I quickly shut the door with my bounty, heart racing a bit as I examined the vacuum cleaner. It was filthy, and the nozzle was broken, but my room was dusty. My allergies were bothering me, so I asked to borrow the vacuum after a nurse had asked me if I had a runny nose. I didn't want to lie and say no. It's a bit silly to assume my dust allergies were COVID, but any symptoms associated with the coronavirus could end up with extra probing and an unnecessary trip to the hospital.

There was a case where a woman had diarrhea on a plane because she had a fear of flying; clearly a case of irritable bowel that flared up with the added stress of travel. Being the honest person she was, she put it down on the travel declaration form, and it caused a frenzy of activity at the airport as she was quickly separated from all the other passengers by hazmat-suited personnel and whisked off to a health hotel. She reported that her accommodation was very comfortable and she was enjoying all the extra attention. If she had been in Perth, where they didn't have health hotels, she would have been put into a COVID hospital ward.

I vacuumed my room and returned it to the hallway so it could circulate amongst other inmates as needed. We were also given other cleaning supplies: dishwashing liquid, cleaning wipes, and laundry detergent. The hotel provided two rolls of toilet paper, which I needed to ration carefully as Australia was suffering a national paranoia over toilet paper shortage. Even NYC, at the time a COVID hot spot, hadn't been quite as TP obsessed. Considering the low incidences of the coronavirus in Australia and that toilet paper was mostly made locally, their attachment to stocking up on bum wad won them the international title of Toilet Paper Hysterics. Angry Aussie shoppers attacked each other over the last roll, often wrestling each other to the ground to claim victory over fears of a dirty tush. To ensure that the community could maintain a clean derriere, newspapers printed blank pages to combat the bog-roll-hoarding issue. Eight full pages of dotted cut-out lines (just in case you had forgotten how wide toilet paper was) to be used in case of a dire emergency.

I imagined myself sitting on the loo, reading the paper, and after I had relieved myself, pawing at an empty toilet roll as it spun around with just a few strands of paper glued onto it. I was stuck in the office hallway bathroom a few months ago and hadn't noticed they were out of butt tissue. I contemplated how I could get out of the messy predicament. As I was calculating my next move and praying for the goods to miraculously manifest, I was visited by the toilet paper fairy, a.k.a. the janitor, who handed me a commercial-sized giant roll. However, it's a little-known fact that the toilet paper fairy only visits once per lifetime, so I grabbed the scissors in my sink drawer and cut out perfectly even strips of toilet paper. It wasn't Angel Soft, but it did the trick. With this knowledge in mind, I anxiously calculated how many squares of toilet paper I could use daily: one hundred and fifty pieces per roll, one roll per week, which was twenty-one per day. Being a woman posed a great toilet paper disadvantage. Pan Pacific communicated to the inmates through Facebook, and they made random announcements daily about free pizza, winning drinks for being able to name local places in Perth and quarantine-related facts. Later in my stay, they announced that extra toilet paper would be provided free of charge, rendering my efforts to practice toilet paper conservation unnecessary.

The quarantine cost was mandatory unless you could show that you had less than $5,000 in your bank account for three months in a row, including the month of travel, as well as a tax return corroborating your no-income story. (Un)fortunately, I wasn't poor enough to qualify for free quarantine. We did not pay the quarantine bill at the end of the two weeks, but an invoice was sent to us about two months later by mail and email. Some people tried to cheat the system and siphoned money into other accounts for a few months but were caught when they were asked to show bank statements two months after the quarantine period. If you were a student and had no money, even if you were considered an adult, your parents were forced to pay your quarantine expenses. There were many people who did qualify for the fee exemption. Some sources, including the Department of Foreign Affairs and Trade (DFAT), said that 90 percent of people who went through quarantine didn't pay or paid a reduced amount. That number seemed inflated to me, considering all the people on Facebook who had reported they had paid the total amount versus those who didn't pay at all.

*****

That first day, I chatted with friends scattered all over the world, whom I had made from my childhood through college and professional connections. I touched base with my closest friends almost daily or every few days—a group of about fifteen people from when I was three years old to more recent years. They were curious to hear about my experience, what the room was like, as well as the quarantine process, and what it was like to travel internationally with COVID restrictions. Staying in touch with my friends helped tremendously with feeling grounded and connected with the rest of the world.

The first twenty-four hours in quarantine felt like an eternity. It was rather mind-numbing. The hours seemed to drag as I watched the minutes slowly tick by. Thirteen more days of this were going to be agony. I posted on the uncensored group asking if they knew anyone who successfully escaped from the hotel. No affirmative responses, but most people had thought about it. I asked what others were doing to pass the time. Half seemed to have been hand washing their laundry and watching it dry, and the other half avoided doing laundry and enjoying the shock value of their abject nudity when the nurses knocked on their doors.

I called my mother—she seemed upbeat and expressed that she was looking forward to seeing me. She asked how I was feeling. I lied and told her I was doing well—I didn't want her to worry. She asked about the kids and how they felt being left back in New York, as they had originally planned to come to Perth with me. Since I had hastened my trip at the last minute, they bumped off the ambiguously empty flight. Since the pandemic, my kids and I have been glued together 24/7. I was secretly happy to be forced to leave them. I was also glad to be able to shield them from the unpleasant experience of this quarantine and witness their grandmother being so ill. They would miss the opportunity to say goodbye to her, for which I hoped they wouldn't resent me. I reassured my mom that her grandkids were OK, immersed in their school schedules and TikTok. She mentioned she looked forward to my cooking. Cooking for her had always given me so much pleasure. I was hoping we would get to have at least a few meals together. She tired quickly, so the conversation wasn't as long as I would have liked, but I was happy to hear her voice.

My sister Etsuko, who lived in Melbourne with her partner and kids, had flown out to take care of our mother for the past five weeks. She had just left and tag-teamed with our middle sister Keiko, who had moved into her place, and the plan was for me to take care of her for a month after I finished quarantine. Unfortunately, my mother's health had declined very rapidly recently, and I was becoming afraid that I may have waited too long and that my time to take care of her would be brief.

I had heard of other Australians returning to Perth only to have their family members pass away while they were in quarantine without even being able to see them. I was concerned that I might fall into that camp. There were thousands of people in the Facebook group whom I had asked about an exemption to visit someone in hospice care. Many had tried, but nobody reported an exemption.

The health department stated that exemptions on compassionate grounds were granted case by case, but it looked like it wasn't an intuitive process that anyone had managed to navigate. Since nobody had actually been given an exemption, I thought pursuing it would be futile until a close elementary friend of mine informed me that a friend of hers had been given an exemption to see their mother. He saw her the day he arrived in quarantine and his mother passed the next day. I wondered if it had been easier for him because he had traveled from New Zealand before the travel bubble, which was still a COVID-free zone. I, on the other hand, was coming from a previous hot spot. In general, U.S. travelers were largely unwelcome; viewed as an oozy, repulsive, large pimple that the government wanted to hide behind a wall of concealer. I started the process of getting an exemption as soon as I settled into the hotel. I understood it would be extremely difficult with many dead ends and emails that fell into the abyss of government wastelands. *Come on, people! My mom's dying! A little help, please!* My silent screams were ignored. Though the government stated that they gave exemptions for compassionate reasons, it just looked like a cheap way to placate the public.

I pulled out my yoga mat and half-heartedly did some poses. I felt uninspired and couldn't focus. I turned on a beginner belly dancing tutorial and tried out some moves. How on earth do they do that shimmy move? My hips didn't move that quickly. I caught myself in the reflection in the window, and it looked like I was having convulsions. The instructor said belly dance was a sensual, feminine dance that's intuitive and natural, so if you felt like you were gripping, then it probably wasn't natural. I glanced at my hands; they looked like chicken feet in shock—probably not the aesthetic the instructor was looking for. Despite the fact I had barely done anything, I was exhausted, and it was time to go to sleep. I went to bed thinking this was horrible, but it could have been much, much worse.

Maybe the universe heard those words and mistakenly took them as a prayer.

DAY TWO

I woke up in a jet-lagged haze to a flurry of texts from my sisters that our mother had fallen and was in the ER. Since Perth was in a three-day lockdown after one positive COVID case in the community, everyone was expected to stay home and only go out for grocery shopping and medical appointments. Keiko was waiting outside the hospital in her car to be updated on whether she had suffered a fracture. She had been woken up at 5 a.m. by our mother huskily calling out for help. She had fallen while trying to go to the bathroom unassisted. Even though Keiko had asked her to wake her up if she had to go, she had put a mattress down in the living room next to our mother's bedroom specifically to help her go to the bathroom. Perhaps it was out of sheer stubbornness that made her believe she could still walk unassisted, or she didn't want to inconvenience my sister, who had been sleeping, but that night my mother had attempted the twenty feet from her bed to the en suite toilet alone.

A million thoughts darted through my mind, including an impulse to kick down my door and make a mad dash out of the hotel to get to my mother, still in my underwear. Considering how clear she had sounded on the phone the previous night, this irrational decision to go to the bathroom unassisted seemed like a worrisome turn of events over a short span of time. My mother's decline yet again felt ominous, and I was consumed with a gripping fear that I wouldn't get to her in time.

My mother was diagnosed with cancer about six weeks after I had heard about her failing kidney transplant on the subway. We briefly celebrated a clean slate of health, but the cancer returned quickly. My sisters and I supported her decision not to treat it and to continue with palliative care. She had already undergone an exhausting kidney transplant and had been sick on and off for over four decades. She had endured multiple medical procedures and surgeries, and her body had suffered the ravages of those ongoing treatments. Her immune system had been compromised by the immunotherapies used to treat her twelve years before. Now cancer had spread aggressively. Her original prognosis had been a year, but fate shortened it expeditiously from a year to six months, to a few months, to a few weeks. Etsuko had asked for a reclinable hospice bed for her home as our mother began having trouble getting in and out.

Unfortunately, those were reserved for people in their last few weeks of life. So, when hospice care offered her the reclining bed without us having to ask for it again, we knew that the prognosis had worsened. That's when I changed my flight. The last time I was in Perth was for the holidays of 2019. Even then, I had planned to see my mother three times in 2020 because I knew that her health was unstable and things could turn for the worse quickly. Planning trips meant, in addition to all the normal prep, arranging care for our pets and finding coverage for my patients—and those were trips on which my children came with me. So, leaving town with only a day's notice had been chaotic, in the drop-everything-and-put-on-unwashed-underwear-inside-out kinda way.

Hours passed as I waited by my phone to hear the news about my mother's fall. My sister made a three-way call from her car. I picked up in a split second, as did Etsuko in Melbourne.

"Mum is OK, there's no fracture," she said. We all exhaled deeply.

Despite the fact that there was no fracture, my mother was in a tremendous amount of pain, so she was admitted to the hospital, although she also asked to be discharged as soon as possible. My sisters and I unanimously agreed it was unlikely she would be discharged ever again. Still, the realization was a painful one. My sisters discussed if we needed to tell our mother the truth. I thought lying would probably be best in this case.

Sometimes being honest is a dumb decision. I don't understand brutally honest people. Should we say, "Nah, this is where you're dying, Bub?" Instead, we said things like, "Let's take it a day at a time, and if your pain improves and you can walk better, we will take you home."

I spoke to my mother for less than a minute after she had been admitted. Her voice sounded coarse, and she complained that her back and leg hurt a lot. I told her to hang in there. "The doctors will give you the right medication," I tried to reassure her, "even if it takes a little while for it to all kick in." I knew there wasn't anything I could specifically do for her, and with the lockdown in place, no visitors were permitted, including my sisters—not to mention me. The barricades between my mom and me had just become ramparts.

I sometimes have this reoccurring nightmare where I'm trying to get somewhere, but I can't move fast enough, and when I eventually get there, the event is over, and nobody is left. I felt like I was caught in my own dream—except that I wasn't dreaming.

As I processed this new development in my mother's health, I got to enjoy some more unpleasantness: I underwent my first COVID test in quarantine. Collecting the specimen in Australia differed from the States. In Australia, they collected saliva from both nostrils and the throat, in that order. And it's not just the rim of the nostril like I had been accustomed to, but far back and deep into what felt like my brain. After they pulled a wobbly booger from my second nostril, still attached to a string of mucus, they put the same long Q-tip into the back of my throat. I hadn't intentionally eaten my own snot since I was about four. I simultaneously gagged and sneezed with my mask down, right in the face of the nurse. Just a friendly spritz that splashed onto the nurse's plastic face shield.

At the end of the mucus violation, the nurses wished me a good stay, promising they would return on day twelve. Since the COVID test results are usually back in twenty-four hours, results would be ready on day thirteen.

They kept everyone on an extra special day...for no reason.

*****

There was a nice-sized TV on which I flipped through channels. Nothing interested me. I mindlessly touched random buttons on the remote without looking at it. I had never been much of a TV person, and it was too loud, which in retrospect, was maybe my fault. Had I not just turned it down? But if that even occurred to me at the moment, I didn't do it. Instead, I grabbed my phone and watched some cat videos for a few minutes, then jumped to makeup tutorials, unsolved crimes, etc. It could have been alien autopsies, and I would have thought, *Yeah, that's just everyday stuff. Boring. Next.* There were several calls from my siblings with updates on how our mother was doing. The hospital struggled to control her pain, so they switched to more hardcore pain management. I knew the side effects of these drugs and that sometimes if they need to give in high amounts, it can complicate breathing. I was concerned that my mother's life would slip away even more quickly with this increased use of morphine. Life is unfair, I know this, but the odds were stacked against me, and I anticipated the unfairness of it all to tip into untenable. I wanted to throw an adult tantrum, but I stopped myself as I didn't have the funds of rockstars to pay for overturned lamps and other broken property.

Meanwhile, my go-to defense mechanism, *attention deficit*, was functioning fantastically. The upside was that I wasn't able to focus on the sheer magnitude of my fragile emotional state and the impending doom. The downside was that I couldn't focus on anything at all. It was too much for me to process, so I got up from fidgeting with my pencils. I had been taking notes about what my sisters had assigned me to do, as I wanted to do as much as possible from the hotel room. My brain moved slowly, and small task completion took a Herculean effort. I got my yoga mat out again, lay down on it, thought about stretching, and forgot what I was doing. Got up and folded my mat up. Got a drink of water. Stood by the window and looked at the clouds. Got my yoga mat out again and asked myself, *Did I just do yoga?* Put my mat down. Lay down on it again. Rolled around without doing any yoga while looking at the clouds. Got up and put my mat away. Got a drink of water. I wasn't even thirsty. I thought, *I should really try to do some yoga,* but I felt insane taking out my mat for the third time in fifteen minutes, so I decided if I waited until tomorrow, I could avoid being certifiably crazy. I nodded to myself, *Tomorrow is good*, I thought finally. Then I got out my yoga mat anyway and laid down.

Hours later, I turned on a belly dancing tutorial and tried to follow along with hip rolls in a figure eight to lighten my spirits. The instructor looked so beautiful—her hips gliding effortlessly in rhythm to the music. I glanced in the mirror and saw someone who looked like she suffered from severe constipation with fingers that seemed to be gripping an invisible hamburger. I had never cared about how terrible a dancer I was. I always just loved it. I wasn't self-conscious about accidentally falling on my ass with my legs spread-eagle like I was waiting for a Pap smear. Improving just a smidge was enough motivation to make me want to go to the next class. A ballet teacher once reminded me that if I gripped my thighs too tightly, I'd do well as a bull rider but not so much as an elegant dancer. I could never dance as she did for the New York City Ballet, but I figured out how to allow the bulls to graze happily in the meadows.

DAY THREE

I rubbed my eyes more than usual in the morning, as everything seemed much blurrier than the day before. It was probably my aging eyes, middle-aged going on eighty, as I blinked several times. As the morning passed and the visibility didn't improve, I flipped through the local news and read there was a bushfire nearby. I was informed to turn off the air conditioner unless I wanted to be smoked out in my room. I had forgotten about the smoggy haze bushfires created.

One of the largest bushfires in Western Australia occurred in the mid-1970s. Smaller bushfires were commonplace. I listened to my father talk about the causes of bushfires in elementary school and, at the time, had been thankful we lived in a suburb where bushfires were unlikely. In third grade, I thought helicopters should be able to carry enough water to put out those fires until he pointed out that those fires were sometimes the size of a small European country.

"How many helicopters do you think you'd need?" he asked me.

I responded, "Many, but can't we just borrow them from all over the world?"

"But they can't just give you a helicopter they may need," he replied. We then had a very sad conversation about what happened to the trees, as well as all the animals.

When my father was in college, he was part of a mountain climbing club. He took groups of young men on weeks-long mountain expeditions in the 1960s. About halfway through one expedition, a man fell from the side of the mountain and crashed to his death. A week away from the base, they had no other option but to cremate their friend's body. My father explained how traumatic this experience had been for him.

Feeling anxious now myself, I focused on the details of the room—described what I saw until my heart rate returned to normal and my anxiety quelled. This grounding exercise helps me when my thoughts are racing and I need to disconnect from perseveration. Focusing on things that have no emotional connection and are mentally neutral stopped my mind from fueling the fire of anxiety.

My room smelled like a cigar lounge. My lungs felt tight, my sinuses were blocked, and my eyes stung slightly. I wore a mask inside and put on my air purifier necklace. According to their advertising, these magic contraptions emit negative ions that adhere to small airborne particulates, adding weight to the pollutants and even viruses, so they drop to the ground, creating a "halo of fresh air." I had bought one to use on the plane as an extra push to keep the coronavirus away.

As a child I had asthma. I no longer needed an inhaler, but I was starting to feel like I could use one now. I loved bonfires on the beach and open fireplaces. Cozying up in a blanket on a cold wintery day. The smoke in those situations conjured fond memories. But the smoke in a hotel room without a functioning window was anything but pleasant. I felt an almost unbearable need to escape creeping up. I sat on my bed, stuffed my air purifier up my nose and visualized myself standing on a beautiful beach.

A man in the uncensored hotel Facebook group posted that he imagined he was in a secluded cabin with an open fire. He even streamed a video of a fireplace to enhance the experience. Genius! We were all being pushed beyond our limits, but I learned that there were additional ways to add humor to my coping mechanisms and to get through these tough days.

The temperature was comfortable without A/C. I wanted to open a window, even knowing that a day like this would probably make things worse. Psychologically speaking, a window that opens is crucial for mental health. But of course, I wasn't allowed to open my windows. I mean, I could throw a chair out the window, but that would probably land me in the psychiatric ward. I wondered if anyone had successfully cracked a window open in desperation.

Given these circumstances, I could see how this scenario would play out. I had read that it is a possible infringement of human rights to not allow people access to fresh air. Considering that outdoor transmission of the virus was negligible, I didn't understand the risk I posed, being on the twentieth floor. That had to be way beyond the social distancing requirements in any country. The only exception would be if a window cleaner was outside and I opened my window really, really slowly as they cleaned it. The opening process would need to take at least fifteen minutes, with the cleaner's nose and mouth inside the crack of my window to become infected. We could also make out, preferably with tongue, to increase the saliva exchange. That would be a better way to catch COVID. But, like I said, I'm a rule follower. And I don't make out with just any window cleaner.

I peeked outside my door to see what they had hurled for breakfast. I caught the staff tossing the food about six feet from the cart, then running through the hallways knocking on all the doors to escape to safety. In the white, plastic trash can liner. I found a stale croissant with a muffin on the side, cereal without milk, and a fruit cup. There was enough sugar to send me into a coma and a meal that showed no effort towards any sort of nutritional balance. I took the food out of the trash liner and left it in a pile outside my door, but I brought in the bag to use later.

Croissants—the freshly baked good ones, not the pathetic excuse for a pastry that they left at my door—were one of my favorite things to eat. Another reoccurring dream I had was of eating a croissant. Biting into the flaky, airy, slightly crisp outer layer into the silky, buttery interior and enjoying the delicious bite melting in my mouth, swallowing it into my empty belly, then realizing holy shit, I'm fucking allergic to croissants and trying to regurgitate it back up. I'd wake up in a panic, one hand halfway down my throat, fishing for the croissant and the other hand searching for my EpiPen.

Australia has always had very strict regulations regarding what food you can bring into the country. Not declaring food to customs and getting caught, one ran the risk of being prosecuted for a criminal offense and, if convicted, could face a penalty of $420,000 or ten years in prison. The list of foods that aren't permitted is vast, including grains, meat, nuts, and even breast milk. To clarify, breast milk that's still in your boobs is OK, but if it's stored after it's been pumped, it may be confiscated. *Sorry, hungry baby.*

When I was still lactating, I planned to go through customs with my Medela Pump in Style double breast pumps attached to my chest, pumping milk while transiting through customs to see if the officers would have the audacity to remove my bags of milk straight off my teats. Unfortunately, my baby had just nursed, so my tank was empty, and I walked through customs with deflated balloons hanging off my chest. What do customs do with all this confiscated food and breast milk? Creamer? There was a time when I was throwing a dinner party, and a dish called for creamer. My creamer had gone rancid, so instead of running out to get another carton, I used my own breast milk. Nobody could tell the difference—or at least that's what I told myself.

I developed mast cell activation syndrome many moons ago. An immune system disorder that was historically overlooked or misdiagnosed. The syndrome   was named in 2007, and at the time considered a rare disorder. It has slowly gained attention. There are several reasons why people develop it. Some are born with it. Patients with long-COVID may develop MCAS too. Mine was triggered by exposure to toxic black mold while living in a "sick" building in Brooklyn shortly after the birth of my first child. A sick building refers to a residential or commercial building where the occupants experience compromised health as a direct link to the time spent in the structure. My first symptom of this disorder felt like food poisoning. My stomach wanted to birth out through my mouth, and my anus was on fire with mini-explosions. Normally, food poisoning might go on for a few hours, maybe a day tops, and you feel like dying, but eventually, most people recover. With mast cell issues, it's like food poisoning never ends. Having never had food allergies in the past, this aversion to most foods came out of seemingly nowhere. One day I ate a bowl of pasta without any issues. The next day the same dish was rejected and ejected from my body within twenty minutes.

It started in my digestive system as cramps, very similar to contractions in labor, but within a few months, I started to develop problems systemically: my heart rate jacked up to double the speed after eating; my blood pressure dropped to the point that I fainted; I broke out into itchy hives; my breathing became labored and wheezy; my sinuses closed over; I had problems swallowing; and on a really bad day, I had seizures. As the symptoms came over me, like an avalanche, all the systems in my body crashed simultaneously. This, accompanied with a sense of doomsday, made my brain decide that a painful and tortured death was imminent.

All these symptoms are caused by my mast cells releasing abnormally high levels of histamines. Mast cells are part of the immune system and play a big role in allergic reactions. If you've ever eaten something and your mouth gets itchy, that's the mast cells releasing histamines. Mast cells are found everywhere in the body, but the predominant histamine reactions occur in the digestive tract, lungs, and on the skin and show up as hives, stomach cramps, difficulty breathing, and sneezing. It can also affect the heart and the nervous system, creating an abnormally fast heart rate, tremors, shaking and, in rare cases like mine, seizures. In extreme cases, it can cause so much swelling that the airways completely close—also known as anaphylactic shock. It is potentially fatal.

An allergic reaction is a way the body protects itself from something it sees as harmful. Sneezing and diarrhea are ways that the body creates extra mucus in order to trap and expel something that the immune system views as dangerous and unwanted. For reasons that are not well known, mast cells can become overly active. When they don't know how to switch off, they keep releasing chemicals. In my case, it felt like my mast cells had post-traumatic stress disorder—they would overreact to triggers that shouldn't be a threat.

It was shocking for me to suddenly not be able to eat 90 percent of my normal diet. Where the diagnosis got trickier and even more misleading was that allergy tests tended to come back negative. Mast cell disease causes food intolerance rather than true allergies. With an allergy, one's immune system creates antibodies when it comes into contact with something it's allergic to. Antibodies directly mediate the allergic reaction. With food intolerance, antibodies are not involved, but rather there's an inability to break down histamines in the body due to an absence of enzymes. With mast cell activation disorder, the mast cells are overly reactive, so whenever the body comes into contact with any histamine-rich food, histamine is released in vast quantities—but my body can't break down histamine.

Mast cell activation is exacerbated by stress thanks to a stress hormone called cortisol, which also causes the release of additional histamines. It took me years to work out what I could eat. I developed post-traumatic stress from not knowing what I could ingest without setting off a reaction. Each time I ate, I never knew if I'd collapse. It was a painful three years of trial and error, with multiple mistakes ending in seizures several times per week, accompanied by severe weight loss. At my lowest, I was 90 lb. at 5 ft., 5 in.

What's worse, invisible illnesses, especially in women, are often treated as psychosomatic. I cannot emphasize the rage I felt when people assumed that I had fabricated my illness to get attention. Like I have nothing better to do, with a full career, children, and personal interests to pursue, than to go see a doctor just to get pity. Most working mothers struggle to even make time for a doctor's appointment. This is the unfortunate assumption that many doctors make about women: If they are unable to find a diagnosis, we must have concocted the disorder in our fannies.

Fewer than a hundred years ago, women were often diagnosed with a case of female hysteria caused by a lack of fornication. A hard penis was the only cure. Men were not predisposed to hysteria as they weren't considered as irritable and lazy. Although we might have come a long way, some of these damaging ideas undermining women suffering illnesses still exist today.

One of the biggest changes in my life after my diagnosis, as a person with family halfway around the world, was the inevitable complication of traveling. Suddenly I had to travel with prepared food.

Airlines offered low-allergen meals, but they remained too

risky. I began to carry lightweight, plastic containers of food in an insulated bag with ice. Whenever possible, I put the food in a fridge and changed the ice when it melted. Going through security at the airport was tricky, as liquids weren't permitted, but JFK let me through with ice. Singapore and Australia did not. The severity of my symptoms has gone up and down considerably, and by about five years ago, I had regained around 70 percent of my typical diet after detoxing mold out of my body, rebuilding my gut biome, and establishing a better blood-brain barrier—all things I spent years studying.

In the months before my return to Australia, my immune system took a hit with the stress of my mother's illness as well as the added complications of COVID. In addition, I was re-exposed to mold in my house. We had had a very rainy season, and unbeknownst to me, a leak in the basement must have been fumigating mold through my house for several months. I didn't actually feel that much more stressed, but my body had been keeping score. I became quite ill. The trifecta of stress had filtered through my mind and been dumped into my body. The variety of food that I could eat decreased to the point that I could only eat a few things without causing a physical collapse of sorts.

By the time I arrived in quarantine, I was only eating brown rice, quinoa, a few vegetables, beef, and chicken. Everything needed to be cooked fresh; no frozen or canned foods were tolerated, and food that was more than two days old caused issues. This was due to the fact that frozen and canned foods are higher in histamines. Leftovers will also increase in histamines the longer they aren't eaten.

Medications and supplements only took the edge off the symptoms but never stopped the physical onslaught from histamine overload. I knew with time, I'd be able to eat more food again, but for now, saying, "Screw you body, I'm gonna eat whatever I want," would land me in the ER, convulsing unconsciously in a seizure, my body propelling substances from every orifice and my airways closing down. After giving birth, I became much more comfortable with my bodily fluids being excreted onto random people, but despite this fact, I didn't want it to happen and definitely not while in quarantine. My fantasy was to waltz through customs, stuffing my face with a bag of potato chips. In reality, this would send me into a coma, and nothing I could eat was permitted through.

I just needed enough food to get me through my first grocery store delivery. I had opened an account to have my groceries delivered before I left New York, but since I didn't yet have a hotel assignment, I couldn't preorder any food. I had to sneak food through customs to tide me over. I had thought about wrapping some food in coffee beans like smugglers hide cocaine. A ten-year prison sentence over a bowl of rice seemed rather harsh, but as Australians say, "Rules are rules." What bothered me was that the same brand of brown rice I was trying to bring in was a brand that was also sold in Australia. When I went through customs in December 2019, I had my beef jerky confiscated, even though it clearly said Aussie beef jerky on the label. I showed the officer. "Look, this was made in Australia, then exported to the U.S., and now I'm bringing it back to Australia." Nope, not OK!

On the plane to Singapore, the flight attendants convinced me to declare my food. If a Singaporean tells you that you need to be careful in a place where you can be arrested for chewing gum, you take this warning seriously. I gave the customs officer my declaration card with the list of all the food that I had with me. He immediately said, "You need to throw that out in the rubbish bin over there. There are absolutely no exceptions to the rule." He got close to my face to make his point. He folded his arms with an authoritarian glare as I tried to argue my case. I explained my condition and even suggested he was willing to let me starve. I sniffled and added a look of despair for good measure. He went to his supervisor and whispered in his ear. The supervisor grimaced, nodded his head once, and shooed him away. "My supervisor said you can take your food." I thanked him loudly and he ushered me away quickly.

Just as well I was cooking my own food, as the fare served at the Pan Pacific was mostly inedible. Military personnel on the Facebook page who knew how to rough it at mealtime even complained that the food was worse at the hotel than rationed portions in remote-area postings. Lunch was burned worms on soggy rice with a side of more rice that was so undercooked it might have actually not been cooked at all. It was tooth-breaking hard, which might be good for someone who wanted to try to swap quarantine for a dentist's chair. One "pudding situation" was unnaturally colored bright pink and resembled something they serve in hospitals for patients who can't eat solid food, layered with a cheese single on top.

I had developed an allergy to most food additives, preservatives, and colorings, and one of the first times, I had a mast cell reaction to a Bolognese sauce I had freshly made. I had just eaten a large bowl of pasta and got into the car to run an errand when the reaction hit, and I was doubled over with pain, severely nauseous, compounded by a panic attack. I crawled back into the apartment and lay shivering in my bed, feeling dizzy and weak, until I lost consciousness. I suspect it was from the red food dye sometimes added to the raw beef to give it that appetizing blood color on the shelf. I'm sorry to say, it turns out most raw beef is supposed to be a dingy brown.

In our cells, I mean rooms, we got regular calls from the medical team, and if necessary, we could have psychologists check in with us daily, as well as a suicide hotline and mental health support 24/7. Mental health issues were one of the most common reasons people in quarantine ended up being transported to the hospital. Most were having severe anxiety and thought they were having a heart attack or suicidal thoughts and psychosis. Apparently, you're five times more likely to end up in the ER due to mental health issues from being in hotel quarantine than if you're at home. The emotional intensity of being locked up for two weeks isn't something to be taken lightly.

In retrospect, I probably should have taken advantage of this free service of psychologists and worked on my related and unrelated issues to hotel quarantine. I could have used the opportunity to process my fears, including a phobia of cheese, *turophobia*. Brie very afraid. Camembert despair. Gouda go potty. I had developed *cibophobia*, a fear of eating any food, not just cheese, although all dairy products were my archenemy for a long time. It's a sad and lonely reality living without the ability to suckle from the udders of cows. Understandably, after everything I ate caused me to collapse, the mind tends to short-circuit in this regard, and each time hunger arrived, so did the fear of another collapse.

The nurses who visited were always very pleasant to talk with and seemed to genuinely care. I asked one nurse if I could stop the meal deliveries, but she said the health department wouldn't agree to it. However, she informed me that the kitchen wasn't reliable in managing food allergies and guests got the wrong food on a regular basis. I was surprised that the nursing staff threw the kitchen under the bus, but was thankful for her honesty. She said, "If I were you, I wouldn't risk eating anything the hotel prepares."

On the third day, I got a call from the hotel chef around 4 p.m., an extremely well-meaning man for someone who considered a cheese single on a pink pile of mush "food." He even had some rudimentary understanding of food allergies. After listening to my story, he said, "How about if I just give you plain quinoa with nothing else."

"In theory, that's OK, but how long will it have been in the fridge?" I responded skeptically.

"No longer than three days," he said, although I wondered if he believed in his own standards.

"Well, my time limit is two days. Food any older tends to give me an allergic reaction." I knew the conversation was a waste of time, but I wanted to be polite.

"I see. How about vegetables? Which ones can you eat?" It felt like he was changing the subject, but I listed them.

"Zucchini, peppers, arugula, green beans, kale, and collard greens." I listed.

"We don't serve any of those in the hotel. Can you eat eggplant, spinach, tomatoes, potatoes?" At this point, he lost all credibility. All those vegetables were high in histamines.

"Maybe we can special order some vegetables for you, but they won't be organic." He had begun to sound a little dejected.

"I have an issue with pesticides, but can eat non-organic vegetables if they are washed well," I offered hopefully.

"Well, I think we can work something out," he said, but his tone said the opposite.

"I appreciate the effort," I responded incongruently.

"I will send you a menu for food delivery options soon." My sense was this was a total lie but a way to end the conversation without claiming defeat.

I thanked the chef for his time and the hotel manager called shortly thereafter. "I spoke to the chef, and I'm happy to report they will do everything possible to accommodate your dietary needs."

"I'm not sure if it's safe for me to eat the food provided by the kitchen," I replied.

"He's a Michelin-trained chef and well-versed in food allergies." I listened as politely as I could. But according to multiple Facebook groups, countless guests who had stayed there hadn't eaten the food provided by the hotel and left it to rot outside their doors.

"I know he means well—" There was no need for me to be rude.

"And how irresponsible it was for the nursing staff to make

such derogatory comments about the kitchen staff," the manager said without letting me finish.

"The kitchen staff isn't medically trained—" I tried to offer as a neutralizing statement, but the manager wasn't listening to me.

"The kitchen will be sending you food soon." He hung up the phone without a closer to the conversation.

I continued to check and see if any special concessions had been made to my meal deliveries, but they just kept sending me food I couldn't eat. Not even one serving of three-day-old quinoa. It bothered me that food was being thrown away every day, even if it was inedible. I grew up in a family where all leftovers were adequately stored and eaten later. We didn't waste any food. My grandparents all grew up during the war and I carried with me their stories of food scarcity. As a child, my maternal grandfather told me he spent an entire week nibbling one chocolate square after the bar had been shared with nine siblings.

Prior to leaving New York, I contacted the Department of Health to request an exemption to quarantine in a place that had a kitchen, explaining the severity of my food allergies. Their response was that all hotels could accommodate any food allergies. Since I had so much free time, I wrote an email to the health department, as well as the local ombudsmen, about my experience. Weeks after the quarantine had ended, I received a reply that they would escalate this matter to the Senate.   Many months later, I received a letter congratulating me on the successful completion of hotel quarantine. The letter ignored my medical condition, and read like a Golden Raspberry Award for completing a challenging obstacle course and avoiding death traps.

Despite the fact that I didn't eat any food that they delivered, I was still required to pay for it. There should have been options to opt-in or out of the meals, maybe looking something like this:

1. All-inclusive menu $900

2. Order from the hotel menu. Prices vary

3. Food delivery from local restaurants. Hotel service fee $100

4. Inedible government-mandated food $400 (not recommended)

Building codes stated that kitchens and bathrooms had to be separated by a wall or a door, so technically, I could have cooked next to my bed, but the only vent was in the bathroom, and the smoke detector was over the bed. I was concerned that I might set off the smoke alarm, especially since there was no vent outside the bathroom. So, I decided to set up my "kitchen" inside the bathroom—the combined room I renamed the *bitchen* where I could shit and stir-fry at the same time.

Cooking without creating any smoke was more of a

challenge than anticipated. I had to learn how to cook everything on low settings. My cuisine was probably on par with what the hotel offered—barely edible—but at least it was something.

One day I noticed smoke coming out of the bathroom. I remembered that I had been sautéing veggies when my phone rang, and I quickly shut the door to keep the smoke inside the bitchen. I immediately turned on the faucet, misted water everywhere, and hand-fanned smoke toward the vent. A smoke alarm going off would trigger a hotel-wide evacuation and might lead to having my cooking equipment confiscated. However, it might have been the perfect quarantine escape plan.

My issues with eating weren't just complicating my quarantine. They had already complicated my relationship with my mother. My mother opened two restaurants when I was in high school, serving Pan-European food at one restaurant and Japanese cuisine at the other. I was given the privilege of illustrating and handwriting the menus. I also worked there as a server. I fell in love with the brioche and stuffed pork tenderloin with prunes my mother served there. The food was immaculate, and with time I even learned how to manage the restaurant. I got to make cocktails when the bar got too busy. One time, a customer ordered a grasshopper cocktail. A grasshopper is supposed to be made with crème de cacao, crème de menthe, and fresh cream, but we didn't have any of those ingredients, so I improvised and mixed Baileys Irish Cream, milk, and green food coloring. Voila! Tasted nothing like a grasshopper, but it was green! The customer didn't notice and, luckily, didn't have mast cell disease.

The point is much of my relationship with my mom revolved around food, so when I developed mast cell disease, I felt like part of our relationship perished. I couldn't eat out at restaurants anymore. I had had too many bad experiences where the kitchen had accidentally added something I couldn't eat. I'd still accompany my family to restaurants, but I wouldn't eat anything—a very isolating experience, sometimes met with judgment. Someone would inevitably say, "This is so delicious, you should try some." The disease became yet another paradigm in my life in which I felt left out and alone and also misunderstood and judged.

Another reaction that many people had was that if I couldn't eat the food they offered me, it was as if I was rejecting them personally. The Buddha died from food poisoning, and my teacher once told me that the Buddha knew he would die after eating spoiled meat, but out of kindness, he ate the food that was offered to him. Maybe eating food that is going to make you very ill is a thing for enlightened folks only.

I called my mom on her direct room line, but she didn't pick up. So I called the nurses' station, and they took the phone to her and held it up. "Oka-San, are you in pain?" I asked, happy to get her on the phone and hear her voice.

"My back still hurts, but it's getting a little better," she responded without enthusiasm.

"I'm sure the doctors will figure out the medication for you soon," I tried to sound optimistic but wondered if I came across as fake. "For now, try to get some rest and I'll see you soon."

"I'm feeling tired, so I'm going to hang up the phone." There was a curtness to her voice that I didn't recognize.

"I understand, Mom. I'll call again soon." Before I finished the sentence, she hung up.

It seemed like her energy had dropped significantly in the last twenty-four hours. *Please, mom, please hold on until I can get out of here.* I could feel her slipping away from me and it was an agonizing experience sitting in my hotel room a short distance away from her. I was tittering next to a slippery slope of despair, about to fall deep into a terrifying memory of being left as an infant and not knowing if I would survive. Rationally, I knew that I would be OK, but my emotions didn't care what was true or not. I told the part of me that felt like I might die that I was going to be OK. It was 2021, and I could take care of myself; I could take care of her, my inner infant still frozen in time.

I closed my eyes and imagined my mom holding me as a

baby and soothing me. My energetic body calmed down. As I stabilized, I took a walk around the emotional pit and examined it some more. It looked very much like a volcanic crater meets scary nightmares and mythical demons. It reeked of death, bubbling and releasing repulsive odors from a sludge mix of green slime, lava, and sewage. And immersed in this disgusting cesspool were dying, creepy old men engulfed with arms stretched out, desperately calling out my name, "Momoko, come here baby and pull me out. Come sit on my lap."

Wanting to uplift my spirits a little, I reached out to a few friends. There have been a number of people I've met throughout my life whom, upon meeting, I felt like I already knew. It was as if our souls recognized each other and we had all met in a distant life in the past. We shared many common interests and senses of humor, and our connection was supportive, kind, and lighthearted.

DAY FOUR

I had spent the last few days trying to demystify the quarantine exemption process. After I got fed up with politely waiting, I emailed every Department of Health–related email address I could find online.

Then, bingo! I finally received a response. In order to process the exemption, I needed to provide documentation from multiple unrelated sources that I had been granted permission to visit my mother during quarantine. They were looking for exacting proof that her death was imminent. One would think a letter from the palliative care physician stating my mother's current condition would suffice, but of course, nothing is supposed to be that simple. I wondered if this was an intentional delay tactic to reduce the number of people who would qualify for an exemption. I'm not surprised very few had made it successfully through the red tape and firewalls, as it was an extremely frustrating process, which cost me a full week to puzzle together. But I persisted. I was relentless. I had come all this way and flown 11,613 miles; I wasn't going to miss out on seeing my mother alive.

In the follow-up email from the health department, it outlined that if an exemption was to be granted, it would be for one thirty-minute visit only, and there would be no more exemptions.

Thirty minutes?! I should have been happy to get something out of this impossible system, but in some ways, it almost felt *worse*. It was harsh. Absolutely inhuman. There must have been better ways to handle keeping the community safe and allowing families to be together, even during these challenging times. What can one say or do in thirty minutes? And what happens if my mother is sleeping during that time? Do I wake her or let her sleep? If I let her sleep, for how long? How many of those precious minutes should I let her sleep away? Should I just hold her hand and chat with her? And what is even left to say? What do you say to someone when you know it's the last thirty minutes you'll ever see them?

I was lucky to have had a great relationship with my mom. I harbored no feelings of resentment or anything that I needed to sort out specifically. My only lingering question was from my childhood when my mother had a tendency to leave food in random places. I'd once found a baked potato in my dresser, a cupcake by the landline phone, and a sandwich in the utility cupboard. I wasn't sure if she would even remember leaving those surprises around. They hadn't been intended as gifts for me, as they were half-eaten. I figured it was just one of my mother's quirks. She'd been eating and gotten distracted. But I stored the question away as something I might ask her about—calculating subconsciously if it was important enough to bring to our last thirty minutes.

Part of the avoidant conversation I was seeking out was

primarily fear-based. I worried I might lose my shit in front of her. During my grandmother's funeral a few years prior, there had been a particularly poignant yet beautiful moment during the funeral service where we were given flowers to place into the open casket. I was overwhelmed with feelings and started to tear up. Not wanting to lose my composure in front of my children, I crouched in the corner of the room to get tissues out of my bag to blot out my tears. With my back turned away from my kids, my mother came to my side quickly and shook her head. I could tell by the look on her face that she didn't want me to cry as she gave me a bunch of beautifully colorful flowers, grabbed my hand, and pulled me to join the flowering ritual. On the other hand, it's possible she just thought I was checking my phone or doing something useless and was upset I wasn't participating. But just in case she wanted me to hold it together, I took deep breaths, choked back my tears, and took a close look at my grandmother's serene face. My mother didn't shed a tear at her own mother's funeral. Perhaps she only did in private. Or maybe not at all.

A day before my grandmother passed away, we had visited her at the hospital. My mother said to her mother, "Hurry up and get better and let's take a fun trip." My grandmother was exhausted and had just told my second cousin that dying is hard work. My grandmother just nodded her head with a smile. From what I could gather, she seemed to be reviewing her life, and when she said anything judgmental, she quickly corrected herself and said, "I must not think in such terms." But when my mother asked her own mother about how to manage a particularly challenging situation with a family member, my grandmother responded, "People are people." What she meant was people are unlikely to change or behave differently. My grandmother seemed to have discovered acceptance in the last days of her life.

My father's end-of-life review was self-critical. He stated how stupid he had been and how much he had forgotten. It was as if he had set out to do or experience something but hadn't completed his mission. I didn't know what he was referring to and I will never find out what he regretted the most about his life.

I wondered if my mother was also working hard to die and what she might review in her life. I hoped she didn't review all the times I got in trouble, including my repeat offenses of keeping a personal snot collection behind the headboard of my bed. I hoped that at the time of my life review, I would look back with only minor regrets. What a win my life would be if I looked back and my only wish was that I had left more snot on the wall.

My mother and I had planned so many trips for the future and I thought about bringing some of those places up. Miracles do happen, and people do recover from the brink of death, so maybe it was best to stay positive or at least pretend that she wasn't dying.

Like many who faced death, she thought she had much more time left, and she shared that she still had work to do on the planet, and it wasn't time for her. So I settled on the vision that I would hold my mom's hand, and she could share with me whatever motherly wisdom she wanted to impart. I would cling to her words and any last stories she wanted to convey. We could chat in any organic way that the conversation would naturally flow, be it places we would visit, the food we'd eat together, or funny memories.

I hypothesized it would be a beautiful goodbye, an opportunity to express my gratitude for everything she had done for me, giving me the freedom to explore and find my path. I knew it would be sad and bittersweet, but a heartfelt send-off for her next adventure to wherever in the universe she might go. I knew I was going to have to keep my shit together for thirty minutes. Maybe I should have thanked the health department for that. Any longer might have been impossible.

Despite my mother having made the decision "do not resuscitate," her palliative care doctor, knowing that I was in quarantine, took the initiative to give my mother another blood transfusion in the hopes she would stay alive so I could see her. By this point, as a side effect of the pain medication she was on, my mother could only nod her head or occasionally say a few words. In her more lucid moments, usually, when the medication was wearing off, she was able to have more of a conversation.

But mostly, she lay quietly.

Since the lockdown was still in effect, scheduled to end in two days, my sister Keiko wasn't visiting her either. I feared my mother would be alone at the time of her passing, which gave me pangs of anxiety. Dying alone, like the fear I had during those many times when I had felt abandoned, was a feeling I didn't want her to go through. But watching her die would be equally gut-wrenching. This dichotomy felt like a piercing knife through my mind and soul, cutting my heart into pieces and pulling me further and further away from my mother and closer and closer to losing my mind. It was too much to contemplate and I retreated back into the numbness of this prosaic space where I didn't have to feel anything.

I opened the door to get another trash liner, leaving the withered, thin, cold quiche, rock-hard bread roll, and some other sludgy thing outside my door. There were no guards in the hallway for me to greet for my daily dosage of human contact. I boiled some chicken and zucchini, then lightly sautéed with sunflower oil to give it some flavor, as boiled chicken cooked in a hotel bathroom is as uninspiring as it sounds and usually as edible as dog food. One time a house guest of mine had unknowingly eaten a box of dog biscuits, thinking they were savory crackers I had left for him. He had gone to the wrong pantry shelf. He reported they had a unique livery taste, and he didn't get sick, nor did he start barking.

My mother and grandmother were both pet lovers. My grandmother visited her dog Cullen's grave every month to give him flowers. My mother called Cullen "Grandma's boyfriend," as whenever he would hump her leg, she would say, "Oh, you're so happy to see me." My mother often talked about her cat that she grew up with when she lived in Wakayama, Japan, as a child. She regretted that she had to leave her cat with neighbors when she moved to Tokyo for her father's work assignment. They had moved into a small apartment that didn't permit pets. Unfortunately, when her family lived there, they had a fire and lost most of their childhood pictures. One photo of my mother with her cat survived. My cat, Zuko, reminded my mother of her cat, and she often asked how he was doing. I had hoped that one day she could meet Zuko in person, as well as all our other four-legged fur babies. I'm sure she would have loved all of them.

DAY FIVE

When I applied for my travel exemption back home to Perth, I needed to provide documentation as to why I wanted to visit. It seemed strange to me, as an Australian citizen born and raised in Perth, that I needed an exemption to travel back home to see my family. Holding an Australian passport made things much easier for me to travel there. If you had family in Australia but were a citizen of another country, things got a lot more complicated. The process for me to return home was relatively straightforward once I worked out what I needed to do. Bringing back my children, who were U.S. citizens, would have meant applying for visas and showing birth certificates to prove my relationship to them.

Truthfully, it was a blessing in disguise that they didn't come with me. Cooped up in one hotel room together would have certainly added to the nightmare. I submitted a letter from my mother's physician, stating her critical condition and was immediately approved to travel. On the website for the G2G Pass to enter Australia, they listed the criteria for documentation, letters from physicians, death certificates, etc., for those traveling for compassionate reasons and in capital letters "DO NOT SEND PICTURES OF DEAD BODIES." A death certificate isn't available until about a month after someone has died, so mourning families, in an attempt to get back to Australia quickly, sent pictures of corpses. I was sure that being a police officer and receiving pictures of dead people wouldn't be pleasant, but waiting a month to get a travel exemption and holding up a funeral for six weeks, couldn't be too great either.

I had left Perth permanently on the hottest day on record, at age seventeen, to pursue a higher education that wasn't available locally—an integrative internal medical program in Eastern and Western medicine in Shanghai. My primary focus was combining pharmaceuticals with herbal medicine to enhance the effects of treatment or to minimize side effects. The main reason why I never returned was that I didn't feel fully accepted or welcomed there. Despite having been born in Perth and never living anywhere else, I was often asked where I was from. I found myself saying random countries as I quickly grew tired of being interrogated about what type of Asian I was. A friend of mine asked me why I didn't tell them the truth. I said if they had asked me about my ancestors, I would have told them Japan. So I asked her, "If I ask you, 'Where are you from?' what would you answer?"

"Perth," she replied.

I went on, "Would you immediately offer to me that you're third-generation Scottish? What if I launched into a conversation about how much I loved eating Haggis?"

As soon as I was back in Perth, I realized little had changed. As I walked through immigration, I was stopped for additional questioning by an officer as all the other white passengers walked by.

"What are you doing here?" she asked.

"I'm visiting family," I replied, knowing where this conversation was heading.

"First time here?" She interrogated me with folded arms.

"No." I felt a ball of anger swell up inside of me.

"When was the last time you were here?" she persisted.

"About a year and a half ago."

She eyed me suspiciously. "Passport, please..." then, "Oh, you're Australian?" She sounded surprised. "Where do you live?"

"America," I said, trying to sound as Australian as possible.

"Do you have an American passport?" she inquired, like I would have been an imposter if I had been a U.S. citizen.

"No, I'm a permanent resident."

"Do you have dual citizenship?" Translation: *What type of Asian are you?*

I explained I was born here and was back to visit my mother, who was about to pass. She quickly closed my passport and gave it back to me, wishing my family well emotionlessly.

Many stranded Australians expressed how they didn't feel welcomed back into their own country. Australia is made up of people from all over the world, yet many still hold onto the "white Australia" sentiment. I found myself feeling a kinship with those people who didn't feel welcomed in their own country despite their ethnic roots. I wondered if maybe this was just a feeling that could be attributed to my not being white. But in actuality, many people didn't feel at home in Western Australia either. Australia started with exiles from their motherland England and her convicts probably never felt welcomed in their new homes either. After all, who feels welcomed or wants to live in prison, no matter how big or beautiful it may be—it's definitely not home. Maybe I had picked up on this ancient energy that still breeds quietly in Australia's ethers.

Perth, to me, is the most exquisite place on the planet; the natural beauty is unparalleled anywhere else I've ever been. The tranquil energy and laid-back vibe make it such an ideal place to relax. It feels like balm to my harried soul after decades of New York City living. However, the looks that I have consistently received from passersby still make me feel uneasy. The xenophobia is palpable and the conservative mentality is often too judgmental for my liking. The minority of open-minded, welcoming people were unfortunately outweighed by the downward glances and remarks of "Go home." I grew tired of micro-aggressive behavior.

Perth was taken over by the British in the early nineteenth century, previously occupied by the Whadjuk Noongar, a local Aboriginal tribe that had inhabited the southwestern part of Western Australia for tens of thousands of years. Perth is known as Boorloo to the native people. Although Australia is a penile colony established by a convict-supportive settlement, WA was the first state that was fully settled by those without balls and chains. A high percentage of those tossed out of England and sent to Australia were convicted for petty crime. Stealing an apple because you were starving landed many young people Down Under. And judging by the strict rules at customs of throwing people in jail for bringing in a bag of brown rice, it doesn't seem like much has changed in the last two hundred years. The frequent number of lockdowns related to the coronavirus (over half a dozen in certain areas) and the vast majority's compliance reflect that Australians continue to hold onto the mentality that everyone still lives in a giant jail cell.

At the time I was in quarantine, Australian polls showed that political support favored stricter border control, and many held strong to the idea that Australia should shut down her borders completely and not permit any international travel on any grounds. For those stuck overseas, the government had given a small window to get back to Australia, but many, mostly for health or compassionate reasons, chose not to travel back during this window.

Those who had no other choice but to stay abroad found that they had difficulty coming home. Ostracized by the Australians who believed they should stay out to keep everyone else safe, even when told that they had been given an opportunity to return, they refused to come back. After reading countless stories of people not being able to return, it became clear that everyone had a unique story and reason why, and this inability to return home had caused immense hardship for them as well as their families who wanted them home.

Australians abroad didn't return home, not because they didn't want to, but because they couldn't. The most common scenarios I heard were when there was a window to travel, they were either too ill, or too pregnant, or they were taking care of a loved one in another part of the world. So, the Australian government asked its citizens to do the impossible: Abandon dying or aging family members. The cold-hearted message that the Australians stranded overseas received was that they were to be blamed for missing the last boat.

*****

I received an email from the health department later that day—the fifth day, although it felt like the fifth month—asking for my boarding passes from my flights from NYC to see if any of the passengers on my flights had turned out to be positive for COVID-19. Fortunately, none had, and I received another email a few hours later stating that I would be given permission to go if I provided another negative COVID test, my fourth test this week.

The email also outlined the guidelines for the thirty-minute visit to the hospital. I was required to change my mask every four hours during my thirty-minute visit, an impossible mathematical equation. I was required to tell everyone that I saw that I might have COVID. I was also not permitted to touch any surfaces. Although I had to change my mask every four hours, I also couldn't remove my mask during the visit. I wanted time to slow down, because thirty minutes would pass in a few blinks. I hoped for the experience to feel like a day-long visit, where I'd need to change my mask at least once. I took the health department's criteria for exemption sincerely and contemplated a serious attempt to follow their instructions. Since I wasn't permitted to touch any surfaces, I would be required to master levitation as I floated through the hospital corridors in a hazmat suit shouting, "I MAY HAVE COVID!" to everyone I passed. I had trouble figuring out how to change a mask without taking it off, but I still had a few days to perfect this task.

3:21 p.m.: I received an email stating the health department would be sending someone to give me a COVID test in the next few hours. Things were finally starting to take shape!

It started to thunder, and a few minutes later, it rained heavily. The cumulative clouds seemed so much closer than usual as the thunder rolled toward Swan River in an easterly direction. The rain cleared the smoke from the bushfire, and for the first time in a few days, I could see the Darling Ranges. The air felt lighter, or maybe it was the relief of knowing that I was steps closer to seeing my mom.

Keiko was also given permission to see my mother, despite the ongoing lockdown, and relayed to her I was coming to see her soon. Keiko had me on the phone when she told her.

"When?" our mother asked.

"Maybe tomorrow or Saturday," Keiko replied.

"Tomorrow seems too far away."

I felt heartbroken. To make it this far and miss my mother by one day or even a few hours. Could life be that cruel? My heart pounded with the injustice of it all. I wanted to scream. All this effort I had put into trying to orchestrate a thirty-minute visit, was about to go to complete waste.

No amount of screaming, no amount of praying, would be heard by the universe. I was stuck in isolation, where nobody could see me and nobody could hear me. I had again regressed to infancy, as a familiar feeling of numbness washed over me. There was no point in trying anymore. A small voice said, "Maybe I don't deserve to see my mom." And the walls of isolation closed in on me, and the light got dimmer.

I found my five-year-old self sitting with arms around her knees, rocking back and forth. She had been sitting outside my school, waiting for our mother to pick her up, and all the other children had already left. There were no teachers supervising. This was the seventies and the norm back then. I sat down beside the little girl in my memory. In my mind, I had done something wrong, so my mother had abandoned me. Maybe my artwork wasn't to her liking, and she didn't like the colors I had used to depict her. I thought her purple face looked beautiful. Or maybe it was because I got a B in spelling. I didn't know what it was that made me so bad that she would leave me.

About thirty minutes later, I saw her car driving over the hill towards the front lawn of the school, where I anxiously waited. I was emotionally exhausted and relieved. I could tell she was agitated, so I couldn't express my anger. But she had forgotten about me. She explained that she hadn't been feeling well, so she had fallen asleep and slept through the alarm. I told her that I got a B in spelling, and she said that I must be a genius because Einstein got all B's too. As I unpacked this memory, it dawned on me that after all these years, I was still operating on an old system. An outdated tape of misperceptions that still played and haunted me. My self-worth had been lost somewhere, and I needed to reclaim it. I didn't need a mammoth amount of self-proclaimed worth, like a U-Haul of my awesomeness. But a little, like a fanny pack amount, just so I remembered I wasn't worthless and was deserving to see my mother.

4:10 p.m.: The nurses arrived to nasally rape me again, taking another chunk out of my brain. This time I managed not to sneeze on the nurse, but I brought up some lunch as they were very intent on poking the back of my throat rigorously. They gave me a bag with twenty pairs of purple gloves for my trip to the hospital. I politely said, "Thank you," but what I really wanted to say was, "I'm the one who may have COVID. What's the point of me wearing the gloves? My hands don't emit COVID. I could sneeze onto my hand, with or without a glove on. It makes no difference. And twenty gloves for a thirty-minute visit? That's asking me to change gloves every 1.5 minutes!" I decided to blow them up as balloons and write "Get better soon" on them for my mom.

DAY SIX

9:19 a.m.: I received an email informing me that I could see my mother today and would be picked up at 10:30 a.m. Excited, nervous, sad, annoyed at myself for not having started the day earlier, I rushed to get out the door on time. I felt elated and immensely fortunate that I was one of the few people who actually got an exemption. Today I felt that thirty minutes was better than nothing! I was optimistic that the visit would go well. I flew around the hotel room to get myself organized for my quick escape into the real world.

Right at 10:30 a.m. I got a call from the hotel asking if I was expecting a van. The hotel operator seemed surprised that I had been given permission to leave. She told me to exit my room and to come down to the lobby. I peered out the threshold of my door and saw a guard standing by the elevator. I waved at him, as I was unsure whether or not he knew I could leave or if he'd try to arrest me. He summoned me over to the elevator.

I was met by a chipper driver and we conversed lightly about COVID and how the Australian government had been handling the pandemic during the fifteen-minute drive to hospital. I also learned about the shortage of fruit pickers in Australia, as borders were closed to migrant workers, and most Australians didn't want to take minimum-wage jobs. I was happy to take my mind off my mom. The fruit rotted on trees, he told me, as grocery store prices skyrocketed. Maybe this explained the shortage of fresh fruits and vegetables in quarantine.

The nurse coordinator whom I had been speaking with for the last week greeted me at the entrance to the hospital; a thoughtful and soft-spoken man, who I hoped also had impeccable bedside manner. We were on the clock the moment I stepped off the van, so after a quick introduction, I launched into a dialogue with him. "The health department wants me to announce to everyone I see that I may have COVID."

With a horrified look on his face, he replied, "Oh my lord, please don't do that, you'll create massive chaos."

"I had a feeling that would be a bad idea," I agreed.

That became my first Department of Health violation as I passed about thirty people walking through the narrow, meandering corridors without telling them that I might have COVID.

I felt for this man who had to deal with the other side of all the bureaucracy. I asked, "How many people have you coordinated a quarantine exemption visit for?"

"Since the pandemic started? Only about twenty." I thought that seemed like a pretty low number considering that this was where people came to die. "That's actually considered high," he said, reading my mind, "because many hospitals don't have a palliative ward."

"Has the process of getting a quarantine exemption changed since the borders opened up?"

"Every time I assisted someone," he said, "the process had changed. It has become more and more restrictive each time." He gave me an example of the last person who hadn't needed three separate letters. The majority of patients passed away while their family members were trying to get the exemption. It was hard for everyone. "How are you coping through all of this?" he finally asked.

"I can't say it has been easy, but I'm hanging in."

I anxiously followed the nurse coordinator through the maze of corridors as he escorted me to my mom's room. He reminded me gently, "It's literally thirty minutes, I'll knock on your door when it's time." He had compassionate eyes.

My mother was sleeping on her left side, with her face visible as I walked in. Her face looked so puffy and her complexion was yellow. She didn't look much like the mother I had last seen. I put my bag with the twenty gloves and the extra masks on a chair and walked to her side. Not wanting to wake her, I put my hand on her shoulder and stroked her arm gently. She fluttered her eyes.

"Hi mom, are you OK?"

She nodded.

"Are you cold?"

She shook her head.

"Can I get you a drink?"

No, she shook.

I stood there quietly for a minute, just with my hand on her shoulder. "Can I give you a massage?"

She shook her head no.

I touched her hand and she said, "Samui," *cold* in Japanese, as she pulled her hand away from me. I put the sheet over her hand and placed my hand on top of hers, which she seemed OK with. I was in shock and I didn't know what to say. My mother couldn't carry on a conversation with me. All the things that I had contemplated discussing were lost to the emptiness and I agonized about how I could connect with her. A pit of growing sadness and frustration brewed in my lower stomach. I stood paralyzed, unable to speak or do anything, and after fifteen minutes, I broke the silence. "Don't worry about us mom, we are going to be OK, and we'll take care of everything like you asked."

She nodded, but it was as if she no longer cared.

When my father passed away thirteen years prior, I had had the opportunity to spend a week with him about a month before he died. He was in the hospital, but he was still very conversational. I have cherished these memories, as it was such an ideal end to our relationship. My father always gave me solid business advice and at the time of his passing, I was in a particularly challenging work situation. He told me that I didn't need to worry about the business mistakes I'd made, because he'd made them too, and if I learned something positive from them, then they weren't mistakes, but something valuable to apply towards life. I have held those conversations close to my heart for all these years and although his loss was sad, his parting words had been uplifting. When I left him, I knew it would be the last time I would see him, but I said I'd fly back to Japan to see him again soon. We both knew this wouldn't be possible, but saying goodbye was too painful. I took a long look at him. I wanted to imprint his smile in my memory as I waved goodbye by the hospital room door. My heart wanted to stay longer as my feet carried me away.

I had wished for a similar experience with my mother—a memorable and heartfelt connection. About twenty minutes into the visit, she finally recognized it was me. I had mentioned my sisters' names and that they would be visiting again soon. That's when she realized, "Ah, it's you, Momo," she said very casually. She referred to me with about as much enthusiasm as if she were reviewing one of my report cards from elementary school.

Etsuko had warned me she might be too tired to show any affection. "Don't take it personally if she is cold."

I didn't want to take it personally, but I kinda did. It was disappointing that her spirit, the loving and thoughtful energy of my mother, had already departed.

The sadness and devastation I was experiencing made the thirty minutes grow almost intolerable. I wanted to leave with time still on the clock. I felt guilty. I had received my wish for the thirty minutes to feel longer. Every minute dragged on, magnifying the heaviness in my chest, and as a mix of emotions hit me, tears started to roll down my face. I grabbed a tissue that was on the table next to my mother near an untouched juice my sister had left. I took off my mask and wiped my face and blew my nose. Oh damn! My second Department of Health violation.

Despite understanding that I may have just hit on a bad thirty minutes for my mother and knowing that my mother's behavior was nothing personal, it didn't help that the shockingly unexpected nature of the visit had made me regress to when I was two years old. I wanted my mother to pick me up, sit me on her lap, and wipe my tears with a tissue. I wanted her to tell me everything was going to be OK, that she may have to go away for a little time, but we would be together soon. I wanted to be mature about this, but I was not. I stood with my adult makeshift bib around my mouth, feeling lost, drooling.

I was silent, but my inner voice was screaming, *Please mom, please open your eyes and see it's me. I'm here, please look at me, connect with me. I came all this way to see you. You can't go without even saying goodbye. Just come back for a minute and let me hold your hand. I miss your spirit, where have you gone?*

I tried to hold her hand through the sheet again, but she said she was cold, and she pulled all the covers over her hands and tucked the blanket under her chin.

The nurse knocked on the door. It was time to leave.

I said just a minute. Then I collected my things and headed towards the door. I reached my hand out to turn the door knob, but then I hesitated as something nagged inside of me. I rushed over to my mother again.

I said, "I promise I'll see you again. I'll be able to see you again, right? We'll meet again sometime soon. Promise to me we'll see each other again."

She nodded several times quickly, her lips pursed, her brows furrowed as her eyes squeezed tightly to hold back her tears. That's when I saw it. Her spirit came back and we connected for a second. I felt my heart open up as she reappeared. But she couldn't sustain the connection, it seemed like it took too much energy and her feelings evaporated like dry ice on water. She shut down again and fell back asleep.

The disappointment crushed me under its weight. It was like trying to catch a bar of soap under water—the more distressed I became as I tried to aggressively grab onto the soap, the further it slipped away, propelling it away from me. My mother moved further and further away as I tried to grasp at straws, falling through the sky without a parachute or a safety net, I descended, crashing into the molten lava of hell. Unlike with my father, I didn't take a deep look at my mother. It was too painful. I hung my head low.

I walked out and I could feel a bunch of eyes on me. *There's the woman who may have COVID*, I guessed they were thinking. I kept my eyes on the ground.

The nurse asked me, "How are you doing? It's so hard, isn't it?"

"Yes, it's so hard. I'm OK. Thank you." I had shut down, I needed to function to get back to the hotel.

The nurse walked me back through the maze of corridors in silence. Quite discombobulated and a little dizzy, I caught my foot on a step and quickly grabbed the handrail to catch myself in a half-split with feet three steps apart. "Oh my, are you OK?" He reached out instinctively, trying to help, but then withdrew his hand quickly.

Others glanced over sideways as I had broken yet another rule—I had touched a surface. My third violation. *Sorry Department of Health.* No doubt the cleaning service would be bleaching, if not detonating with explosives, every surface I had come into contact with as soon as I departed anyway. I was surprised nobody had followed behind me with disinfectant spray. The nurse and I stood outside the hospital as we waited for the van to pull up.

"Has anyone visited twice?" I asked.

"No, unfortunately not."

The van arrived and I got inside. "I hope you get to spend more time with your mother," he said kindly.

I knew he knew this wouldn't be possible.

*****

Upon my return, I was met by five security guards. They created a human barricade for me to enter the hotel. The driver warned me, "They treat you like you're wearing a bomb."

I fake laughed, "I'm enjoying this special treatment."

I was escorted out of the car, feeling like a celebrity, as I entered the hotel. I overheard a guard mumble into the walkie-talkie, "She is inside the hotel."

The hotel coordinator stood back against the wall and pointed, "The key card is on the countertop."

"I brought mine from the first day," I answered.

"The card is programmed to be used once only." Apparently, many have tried to sneak out at night and have found they couldn't get back in.

I walked back into my room. *Eight more days,* I thought. Nothing much to look forward to now. Just having to go through the impending death of my mom in isolation. I walked into my room and it felt even smaller than before. Drained and depressed, I slumped down onto the chair and gazed outside. It was a beautiful day; the pristine blue sky with little, puffy clouds put me into a peaceful, meditative state.

The rest of the day, I was an emotional yo-yo. Sad, angry, depressed, anxious, afraid. Like a ball inside a pinball machine, I erratically bounced around, sometimes setting off bells and alarms. Little did I know that a new high score of emotional pinball from this day would be easily shattered in the coming few days, multiple times over.

It's not easy having a mind, a body, and emotions to manage. My emotions dominated that day, but it was not as if my body's needs could stop.

My body knocked at my mind. "Hello? Ahem…kinda hungry over here."

"What? You need to eat again? Can't that wait until we are finished dealing with this emotional crisis?"

On days like this, self-care for me was a by-the-minute evaluation. What did I need right in the minute to basically get through? A cup of tea? A talk with a friend? To just lie down and stare at the ceiling? Maybe I needed to watch videos and try to take an emotional hiatus. Or maybe I needed to research getting a lobotomy.

The hardest thing was nurturing the part of me that felt like I wouldn't survive after losing my mother. I think no matter how old we are, we are still our mother's baby and that bond at risk of being severed had me feeling like my survival was at stake. Dialoging with that part was probably the most helpful thing in the moment, just to remind myself that I was now an adult and we would be OK whenever it was time for Mom to leave. The baby aspect in me was particularly active and there were moments when the panic of impending abandonment was so intense I wanted to stick a whiskey-dipped pacifier in her mouth and call it good. Pity for my allergies, otherwise, I would have been on a third bottle of booze that day.

But of course, I couldn't rely on any substances or medication to numb myself, although a horse tranquilizer would have been welcomed. I was forced to dig deep into all the coping mechanisms I had collected through the psychology programs I had taken and any others acquired throughout my life.

There are two types of coping mechanisms. They fall into either "healthy" or "unhealthy" categories. For example, getting shitfaced drunk may serve its purpose of taking the edge off, but it's not necessarily *good for you.*

I wanted to engage in the healthy alternatives, since my body had trouble processing lunch—much less drugs and alcohol. But those weren't the only unhealthy coping options available to me. There are also forms of "unconscious" coping. Meaning that many of us are unaware of when we have entered into a coping strategy.

There are many defense mechanisms, which were first identified by Sigmund Freud. Here are ten commonly recognized ones:

1. Denial
2. Repression
3. Regression
4. Rationalization
5. Avoidance
6. Reaction Formation
7. Dissociation
8. Intellectualization
9. Compartmentalization
10. Projection

Some of the ones that I have historically visited are *repression* and *intellectualization.* I explored *denial* thoroughly through quarantine and as a child I probably *dissociated* during traumatic experiences. Denial is one of those interesting coping mechanisms because too much of it will distort reality, but there's a time and place for it, and some studies have shown that it can improve survival rates. One showed that the survival rate for cancer was higher for patients who were optimistic about their recovery, as well as those who were in denial about their cancer.

We all have our favorite defense mechanisms, our default coping strategies, much like our comfort foods. They're OK in small doses, sometimes even necessary, as long as we agree that they are often unhealthy in large amounts.

I wanted all of my defense mechanisms in top working order for me to survive this experience in hell, while knowing that I would need to process everything that was shelved at a later date if I wanted to regain balance.

Intellectualization is when I rationalize and use logic to deter myself from my feelings. For example, when I was visiting my mother, if I had rationally concluded that my mother was unable to connect with me as she was sedated, that would have been a use of intellectualization. However, I went into another defense mechanism, regression, where I became a much younger version of myself.

The thing about a coping mechanism that's often misunderstood, is that even if yours includes a tornado-proof umbrella and an inflatable steel canoe, it doesn't necessarily mean that you are coping *well*. You might feel a little better in the moment. You might function a tad better, and feel like an ounce of burden has been lifted off your shoulders, but it's not always sustainable. For me, it's important to try to make myself feel better; to put a layer of balm on my emotional wounds, even if that means that I only have a drop to apply to a Grand Canyon-sized weeping sore.

A few years ago, I lost one of my best friends. She was in her early forties and left two small children behind. She had lost an eighteen-month battle with cancer and, while in hospice care, passed away without any family or close friends by her side. I was angry. I couldn't understand why life gave some women children they couldn't raise. I think anger and sadness are appropriate in situations like that. We might even struggle to cope.

After my best friend died, it would have been a long stretch for me to cope amazingly well. It would have been an impossible feat for me to have smiled every day and gone on with my daily responsibilities as if somehow my life had been gloriously enriched by her loss. I had been grieving her for a long time. In fact, I knew something was very wrong when I saw her just before she was diagnosed, and she looked six months pregnant. I urged her to get checked out, but she assured me she was just bloated. It was only when she collapsed after a coughing fit a month later and was rushed to the ER that she was diagnosed with stage four cancer. She went down a similar treatment path to my mother until she developed resistance to chemotherapy. I visited her as much as my schedule would permit, which never felt like enough. As I watched her slip away from me, I wasn't coping gracefully.

A chunk of my heart went missing when she died. I was too busy to collapse from grief. I went to work, I cared for my children, and I called up all my coping mechanisms to make it through those tough times. I went into coping mechanisms hyperdrive and developed a case of Pollyanna Syndrome for a while before I managed a better balance processing grief. Coping mechanisms aren't intended to make the dark crevices of the asshole squeaky clean and beautiful, they are just that extra square of toilet paper to wipe your shit. It's a course correction, or minimally speaking, it can lead us one step in a better direction. And that step might mean the difference between getting through quarantine or swan diving out a window. And when faced with a crisis, it's comforting to know that you are ready and armed with sufficient toilet paper.

I experience trauma, like many things in life, as a spectrum. I think to some extent, by the time we are adults, we have all brushed up against some form of trauma. And how we handle it is an individualized and personal process, with some people coming out stronger, or at least higher functioning, and others not fairing as well and being emotionally crippled for life. There was no way that I was going to make it through quarantine, skipping with joy through daffodil-filled meadows. It was going to leave at least a few scars. My intention was to survive quarantine, to do as much damage control as possible, and minimize the potentiality of trauma.

From everything I have researched, both professionally and personally, the impact of trauma is not quantifiable. In other words, two people can go through similar trauma and have polar opposite reactions, or two people experiencing different traumas—one that may appear objectively "not so bad" and another that looks more extreme—may have a similar reaction.

To give you an example, there was a patient whom I had seen for quite some time. Her trauma about being separated from her wealthy family and marrying someone with less wealth, often left her visibly distraught. She once came to me crying over the fact that they couldn't stay at the Four Seasons on her next vacation.

Another patient that same week was a young mother who had been taken from her abusive parents and placed in the foster system. She talked about how the trauma had made her stronger and how she never took anything for granted. She was stoic and calm, as she reasoned through her pain.

It's not the outer experience, but the inner constructs of various coping mechanisms that seem to determine one's ability to process traumatic events and to move forward with less impact. The spectrum of trauma that we may find ourselves in, may even be defined by how much it hinders our ability to live our lives. How much does it consume and distract us from focusing on what we want or need? What I really wanted was to fast forward a few months, so I could be back in my house surrounded by my friends, family, and a familiar schedule. But JFK refused to let me check-in my time machine, so here I was, stuck in the present.

The dread I felt about my last week in quarantine was oppressive at times. I did whatever I could to try to distract myself. I spent some time future projecting and seeing myself at home, reunited with my kids and surrounded by my fur babies. I visualized my bright future where things were in balance again to the best of my ability, as the magnetic pull back into darkness was quite strong. My life wouldn't look the same, but a new normal would take its place, and I wanted to expect good things to happen, to anticipate a miracle.

DAY SEVEN

The sixth day had been a rough one. By day's end, I found myself in denial and deciding that my mother would get better.

This had all been a huge mistake. She was going to get better and I would see her again when I got out of quarantine the next week. I'd finally get an opportunity to connect with her. I began thinking about where we would eventually travel together and all the places we would visit, the dance classes that we would take together, and the fun we would have exploring the world.

I was fully fledged into my own fantasy of spending quality time with my mother when I received a message from the palliative care doctor. Things were declining rapidly. They felt she now had twenty-four to forty-eight hours.

Keiko and her seven-year-old daughter called me from my mother's bedside. My mother recognized both of them and even asked how her granddaughter was doing. I was caught off guard by feeling immense jealousy that she had been able to put together a sentence for my niece, but not for me. I knew I was being petty, but I was unable to stop myself from throwing a short pity party.

Anguished not to be at her side, I thought of ways I could escape to see her. I had learned how to rappel in high school—

maybe the sporting goods store had the right equipment and could have it express shipped. It would probably get confiscated by the hotel staff since they inspect all packages...so...not a good idea.

Maybe I could bribe one of the guards, and he could sneak me out at night, duct tape the door to prevent it from locking. But hang on, no duct tape. I could wedge a tampon in the latch plate hole, then cover it with a panty liner. That should be fool proof....

The reality was that a run out of the hotel room could cost me $66,000 in fines or five years in prison, so I would have to come up with something better. Whilst stewing in my insanity, I received a call from the nursing staff to check on me and see how I was managing in general. The caller was a soft-spoken woman with endless compassion in her voice. I told her about my trip to the hospital, but left out the part about formulating a plan to make a run for it. She probably heard the crazy in my intonations and offered additional counseling services, which I denied.

I'm not against counseling, but the sheer effort for me to talk about anything seemed too much. It was easier to push things down and deal with them later. This would be considered *avoidance* in terms of defense mechanisms. Avoidance in the long term, much like denial, isn't a permanent solution, but in a crisis like I was faced with, it was probably appropriate. I knew I'd eventually have to process the quarantine experience—just not today.

So, with the nurse, rather than unpacking the giant elephant in the room, I quickly changed the subject to how the mini fridge was not keeping my food cold enough, and how I could get a replacement. She explained that the mini fridge actually wasn't a real fridge, but was considered a cooler, which didn't sustain proper temperatures for food safety, confirming the ugly thought I had had the first day. I had already been feeling a little off, but wanted to chalk it up to stress. *Hey, Denial, old buddy!* Now I realized that my food had probably gone a little rancid in the cooler, mistaken for a fridge.

Histamine levels can go up exponentially in unsafe temperatures. This was a huge red flag for my medical condition, but I tried to stay calm. I asked her if I could get a proper fridge and she said the most they could offer was another cooler. What would I do with two of the same coolers, neither of which functioned properly? Two wrong coolers don't make one right fridge. She explained that real fridges take up too much electricity, so they don't offer them. Since this was a matter of my health, I would have gladly paid the few extra bucks to pay the electrical bill. But even that offer was refused.

*****

After hearing the news about my mother's decline, Etsuko came in from Melbourne. I was told she recognized Etsuko when

113

she walked into her room and they were able to have a short conversation.

I dipped into *intellectualization* as I consoled myself by figuring I must have caught my mother at the most unfortunate moment yesterday, after she had just been given her pain medication and was drugged out of her mind. Regardless, I felt left out; unimportant and unworthy. In the past, whenever I called my mother on the phone, she was always so excited to just hear my voice. I missed that so much—the joy it gave me to hear her happy voice.

Maybe seeing her again would just be more of the same painful experience from yesterday. Trying to connect with someone who was no longer there. I equated it to after a breakup: You want hopelessly to see an ex again, but know that seeing them won't necessarily make you feel better, it would just prolong the pain of the breakup and be a reminder of the connection that had faded. I tried to convince myself that it would just make me feel worse. Really, I was just trying to accept the awful situation at hand.

The bonds we create often feel like strings that reach out from our hearts and tie us together. Those bonds can be family and friends, anyone we love. I'm not referring to romantic love, infatuation, or lust, but rather universal love, which can be part of romantic love and can transform from lust. I think many people confuse chemistry and attraction with love. I also think there's confusion between bonds and love, as not all bonds are healthy and based on love.

Usually, love takes time to strengthen over many years. Each time we allow someone to love us and we love them back, our bond is reaffirmed or strengthened. When we break up with someone, or lose someone we love, the strings that tie us together become severed and I think this is what feels so painful. We reach out with our heart strings, but there is nowhere for these delicate tentacles of energy to land anymore and we feel lost. After time, the strings of love come back inside us—it's like they recoil. Even though there was loss and there was pain, if we are able to fully grieve the loss (which isn't to say that we won't ever miss them), the acute and immense pain dissipates. Eventually, what is left is a strength of heart and a greater capacity to love, and within the shadows of the loss lies resilience.

As my mother lay dying, so close to me, and yet so far, having an intellectual awareness of those previous experiences and knowing that my mind and heart would heal, gave me only the most minimal comfort. My mother dying felt like a part of me was dying too. She created me and was the one who gave me everything I ever needed. She was no longer able to give me anything at all. Time would heal this pain, but for now, I had to go through a really hurtful phase of heartbreak. Stuck in quarantine, there was literally nowhere to run. There were no distractions and the intensity of my grief felt magnified. I felt sick to my stomach and wanted to crawl out of my own skin to escape.

I went in and out of claustrophobia, trapped in the small room without even a sliver of fresh air. This was something new for me. But I got a glimpse into this awful feeling of wanting to break free from the four walls into open space. The walls felt like they were caving in and the room was getting smaller and smaller as if an internal emergency alarm had been activated that was flashing red and screaming, "Get out of here! Danger! Danger!" I was in fight-or-flight and I needed to get back into rest-and-digest. There were moments of calm, but the majority of the day was a struggle.

My mom once told me everything is not supposed to be "happy-happy" all the time. That's not life. So I was in one of those *not* happy-happy moments. Being raised Buddhist, I had been taught that there are only a few truths to life and one of those is that things will change.

This too shall pass, I reminded myself. *This too shall pass. Please dear lord, let it pass real fast.* Just ripping off a Band-Aid didn't capture the magnitude of the wounds I felt. I'd also need to rip off Icy Hot lidocaine patches covering my entire body, as well as a Brazilian wax. I wanted to rip everything off right here and now just to get this over and done with.

4 p.m.: Mark McGowan, Premier of Western Australia,

announced that there was a positive coronavirus case at my hotel. A traveler from the United States had tested positive on the second day, and a guard tested positive a few days later. The guard had carried it out to the community. It must have been the guard who I had caught with his mask down. Maybe his pants had come down too. I immediately received texts from several people, hoping that person from the U.S. wasn't me. It was announced that WA might be heading into the second lockdown in a week.

5 p.m.: I received my third COVID test while in quarantine. Out of curiosity, I asked the hotel manager which floor the positive case was on, but he wasn't permitted to tell me. They were testing the entire hotel as a precaution. In the U.S., a potential exposure meant you had been within six feet of someone, both without masks, for fifteen minutes. Towards the last quarter of 2021, an exposure included masked exposures too, but still within six feet. It defied logic to test people who were ten floors away from the person who tested positive, but the paranoia seemed to have eradicated common sense.

DAY EIGHT

For about a year after I first developed the mast cell disorder, all I could stomach were rice and lentils. Everything else made me extremely ill. It took six years to slowly recover 70 percent of my diet. I was never able to eat seafood, fruit, and a few other things, but in general, I was able to enjoy many foods again. When the pandemic hit, almost everybody's life was thrown into chaos. The stress of homeschooling children and trying to manage a small business—not to mention the concerns about the illness itself—was all very challenging to my health, as it was to many. I experienced a worsening of my mast cell disorder and discovered that overnight I had become allergic to many foods again. I wasn't back to eating rice and lentils, but had become allergic to gluten, dairy, sugar, alcohol, pork, eggs...the list went on. I scaled down my diet to a bare minimum of foods, hoping I wouldn't require any medication (as the side effects were often intolerable), if I stuck to my diet. I put myself on supplements to slowly reverse my condition, similar to what I had taken years ago when I first began to heal my body. Unfortunately, due to the constant level of stress, I knew it would take months, if not years.

That day, I cooked some of the usual brown rice, kale, and chicken. However, I started to have an allergic reaction within a few minutes of eating. My sinuses and ears began to fill with mucus. I could literally feel my ears closing up, creating an internal echo. My lungs felt tight and it was becoming difficult to breathe. My face and body started to feel numb and tingly, usually precursors to a seizure. My skin began turning red and itchy. I felt faint and dizzy, like I was going to pass out.

My sitting heart rate was 130; my typical resting heart rate is around 60; the range for an adult's normal heart rate is 60–100. When my heart rate is about 100, it feels like I'm moderately exercising. At 130, it feels like I'm pushing myself. I felt a sense of gloom and panic, both symptoms associated with high histamine levels. I couldn't take any more supplements as I had maxed out on them already, and I didn't have an inhaler, EpiPen, or other medication. Not having had an asthma attack in over a decade, nor a seizure, I hadn't brought any medication and was not prepared for such a severe onslaught of symptoms.

I called the nursing staff immediately to let them know and got a call back from the doctor within fifteen minutes. She coincidentally had just been reading about mast cell disorders and was quite knowledgeable about my condition, which is fairly uncommon as until recently was mostly unknown. She asked me if I had ever taken any antihistamine medication in the past. I said yes, one I did well with and the other to which I had had a bad reaction. I couldn't remember which one helped and which one caused an issue. We looked up the medications together, but my brain fog was so severe from my emotional state, as well as a side effect of too many histamines, that I had trouble focusing. We narrowed it down and then hoped we were right that the medication she was ordering would be the medication that I responded well to.

I assumed that the food must have gone rancid, but I had just received a fresh delivery the day before, so that seemed unlikely. I decided to buy new groceries just in case, and as I was clearing out the fridge, I noticed that one of the bags of green beans was already moldy. Mold spreads quickly when it releases spores, and it must have contaminated everything in the not-cold-enough cooler. I felt panicked and defeated. Mold was my nemesis and what I was most severely allergic to. I cowered in anticipation of what might happen to me with this recent re-exposure to mold. I couldn't afford to take many more steps backwards in my health.

I wrote an email to the health department about my condition and begged them to provide a better fridge. Without any response, I got a knock on my door at a non-meal time, which was within a few hours of sending my email, and I found a small fridge outside my door. A small fridge is still pretty heavy, especially without any wheels to drag it from the hallway into my room. I felt my back go out with the weight. Ugh, just what I needed right now. Hobbling around, I felt like an old, frail lady. I was feeling so sick that I wasn't sure at this point if I wouldn't die before my mother.

The antihistamine arrived from the pharmacy a few hours later. I said a little prayer, "Dear God, I've been a really good girl, and if this is the only wish I'm granted, hang on, you're God, not a genie... anyway God, please let this be the right medication."

I took a quarter of the pill. My body felt stiff from the anxiety. I was in deer-in-headlights mode, anticipating a truckload of symptoms crashing into me. Searing pain and DEATH. I checked in with the medical team on standby in case I needed a hospital transfer. For mast cell disorders, a quarter of an antihistamine pill is like trying to fight a nuclear invasion with a plastic knife. It won't have much effect. However, a quarter of a pill that I'm allergic to, while already in an acute histamine state, is like combining a nuclear invasion with a hydrogen bomb. It was potential physical annihilation. I paced around anxiously. Drank more water to try to minimize a potential allergic reaction. Twenty minutes passed and nothing had changed. Phew! I decided to wait a while before taking the rest of the pill.

I tried to eat a tablespoon of rice for dinner, but my face started to go numb and tingly within seconds of eating it. I took the rest of the pill. This had happened in the past too, when my system had become so weakened or stressed that even the smallest amount of any food triggered an allergic reaction. Mast cells also release histamine under stress, so I was already saturated with histamine. My body had become hypersensitive, and all the stress had pushed it over the edge. I decided not to eat anything else for the day and sipped on some herbal tea instead.

I knew that sometimes even tea could trigger a reaction, but the turmeric tea seemed to be agreeing with me. I felt exhausted, but adrenaline was pumping through my body, making it impossible to rest. Lying down seemed to exasperate my symptoms anyway. I continued to feel panicky, with my heart rate consistently over 100 and I'm sure my blood pressure was rock-bottom low as I hadn't eaten. I was so dizzy I thought I would faint. My body started to shake, which typically in the past turned into a seizure. I had to get myself out of panic mode quickly, as I was on the cusp of a medical emergency. I called a friend, but any sound was too much to process, so I got off the phone quickly. I texted back and forth with a few people and asked that they send me healing energy. A thought to do Qigong came to mind, which I hadn't fully practiced in over a decade.

Qigong is a method of traditional Chinese exercise that combines breath work with movement and meditation. I studied it when I was going to medical school in Shanghai. Medical Qigong is a treatment modality that many terminally ill patients who may have run out of drug therapies turn to. It has significant health benefits and can prolong life. In some cases, it can cure what is considered incurable. I breathed deeply and did some very basic exercises. I slowed down my breathing and focused on centering myself as I stood in a half-standing, half-seated position and gently moved to facilitate the flow of Qi, loosely translated as *energy,* through my body. I continued until my heart rate finally dropped below 100. It was still high, but not disastrously so.

Throughout the rest of the day, my heart rate fluctuated between 90 and 125, and I continued to have anxiety attacks, mixed with migrating numbness and tingling throughout my whole body. There were intermittent shaking episodes, nausea, abdominal pain, and cramping; my butthole felt like it would fall out; light and sound sensitivity that triggered a migraine; and weakness throughout my body. My chest was feeling very tight and breathing was often difficult too. It was as if my body was making the loss of my mother something present and tangible. The chaos I had been feeling on an emotional level had now manifested in me physically. I felt absolutely awful. My histamine levels were probably still sky-high. I took the maximum safe amount of antihistamines, but it wasn't enough. I needed to give my body the time to reset without re-triggering any symptoms. Not eating caused low blood sugar too, but it was better than risking eating anything that would cause a seizure, any part of my airways to close, or unrelenting vomiting. I checked in with the medical team a few times again, reporting on how I was doing. I could hear the concern in their voices. It was an absolutely horrifying experience. I'm not sure how I made it through quarantine alive.

This process of scaling back my diet to the bare minimum and then building it back up again, was something I had done dozens of times since developing mast cell disorder. The trick was when to add new foods and how much. It wasn't like all of a sudden, I could start eating normally. I could add one new item of food back, at most, every four days. Four days was the quickest, but it often took weeks, even months, to introduce new foods. If I had a bad reaction, I had to wait until my system was back to baseline before trying something new again. It was a slippery slope to recovery, with guaranteed mistakes along the way. It was always scary, but I'd learned to manage it without copious ER visits. The difficult part of this rebuilding phase was that the order in which I could add foods back in hadn't been consistent. I couldn't say why this was and why foods that I once could eat, I no longer could and vice versa. The foods that were safe in the past could no longer be my fallback plan. For example, white rice was always something I knew I could rely on. Now just eating a tablespoon of white rice was doubling my heart rate. In the past, I hadn't been able to eat any whole grains as it created so much pain in my belly, but lately, the only grain that didn't make my heart excited was brown basmati rice, which was, incidentally, no longer painful. It was an enigma and as different systems healed at different rates, and other systems were compromised, my diet became a trial-and-error reintroduction.

What I usually did was first smell the food to see if I reacted to the aroma. If my sinuses started to close up with a whiff, then I already knew it would be trouble if I ate it. If it passed the smell test, then I took one bite and waited twenty minutes, because that's usually how long it took for my mast cells to start spitting out histamines. Then I'd take a slightly larger bite of this newly introduced food and wait another day to see if I had another reaction. If my skin didn't react, then the next day, I'd take a slightly bigger bite of the same food. I repeated this technique for four days waiting for any new reactions. And by the end of the trial period of four to five days, if I was OK, then I'd try something new to add. I preferred to wait a week, because sometimes there were delayed reactions. If I was under a lot of stress, then I needed to slow down the process even more.

It was a delicate balance and no method was standard, but keen observational skills and self-awareness were crucial to avoiding a histamine overload. I was not always perfect and the process was frustrating. There were incidences when I introduced foods without using my technique and it turned out fine. Once, I added potatoes with onions and new spices without incident. I admit to having tasted too much of the ice cream that my kids were eating. Sometimes it was fine, and other times it backfired, and I got sick. I'd be left yelling at myself, "I should have known better." It was the same mistake over and over again. When will I ever learn? I knew I had a long road ahead of me to rebuild my diet again. It was exhausting to think about, but there were no other options.

*****

That day, I didn't have the wherewithal to have much contact with my sisters and mother. By bedtime, my system had calmed down a little. I called them. They were both staying with our mother at the hospital that night. It was likely our mother would pass. There was only enough space for one extra bed and they joked that they would sleep head-to-toe in the tiny cot. "No guarantee I wouldn't fart in your face!" Etsuko said to Keiko as they laughed out loud. My mother scolded them in her stern mother voice, "Urusai! (*Too loud!*) The two of you, it's no time to be making these types of jokes!" It made me giggle that our mother hadn't lost her sense of humor.

Our mother was often full of funny stories. Not so long ago, she told me about a colonoscopy she'd undergone in Japan at a teaching hospital. In Japan, colonoscopies are performed while a patient is conscious, without any sedatives. The doctor asked if it was OK if students observed. A little uncomfortable, she said yes, thinking maybe there would be two at most. But in came a dozen or so young students who crammed into the small examination room. She was given a gown with a huge hole where her butt protruded out of the opening. She lay down on her side, butt facing her audience. The doctor explained that he would fill up her bottom with air to get a better look inside. The procedure went smoothly and the doctor explained, "As I take out this speculum, the air will release too." And before he finished the sentence, in the serious clinical silence, my mother let out a minute-long, Guinness World Records–loud fart. My mother apologized to the doctor profusely, as the gas eruption finally stopped. Next, he pressed on her belly, releasing several more short toots.

"I think that was everything," he said.

I was really going to miss her stories.

DAY NINE

My mother made it through the night, her breathing becoming increasingly shallow while having constant tremors. I also made it through the night, but I woke multiple times, my belly aching and my bladder overly active. Still totally shaken from my allergic reaction, I was less focused than I might have been about what was going on with my mother.

Etsuko called to tell me that our mom had been up in the middle of the night and called out my name. She held Etsuko's hand and she seemed comforted by that. It was bittersweet to hear that she had called out for me—only two miles away from her, yet separated by a wall of bureaucracy. I visualized myself sitting in the room with her and holding her hand, giving her whatever comfort I could. My spirit had been shattered and my energy leached out, just trying to get through the minutes. There wasn't a way I could be offering comfort to anyone at this point. Maybe it was for the best I was locked up, even if being locked up had gotten me into this mess to begin with.

I made some quinoa for breakfast, but after one bite, my face started to feel numb and tingly and my ears started to close over again. I still wasn't out of the woods regarding triggering an anaphylactic reaction. My anxiety was intense. I didn't want to lose consciousness and not be able to get to the phone, as anaphylactic reactions and seizures tend to come on quickly. I called the nurse to update her and to let her know that I had already maxed out on all my medications and supplements. The doctor then called to suggest that if I wasn't able to make it to the phone in time, I should yell for help without opening the door. Hopefully, the guard outside would hear; the guards weren't always there. Whenever I opened the door to get a delivery or put out the trash, I was more likely to see an empty seat than a guard sitting there on their phone.

I was warned that opening the door and collapsing in the hallway would be considered breaking out of quarantine and I would be fined. She cautioned me against having a seizure outside my room. The fear of just having a seizure was difficult enough, let alone the possible breach of quarantine for trying to get medical help—it was beyond irrational. The nurse said if I had a seizure with the door open without any part of my body crossing over the threshold of the door, then technically, I wouldn't be fined. *But not a hair over, god forbid, a whole finger.* It would be $6000 for breaching quarantine!

I'd heard some neurologists say that having a seizure alone isn't harmful. It's a way for the body to reset itself. They obviously hadn't had seizures themselves, because it didn't feel harmless when it was happening to me. It felt like my brain and body were getting fried and resembled nothing close to a calming reset experience. It was like a total-body collapse and loss of control as all my muscles contracted and released without my consent, along with pain, nausea, and often loss of vision.

The uphill struggle for my body to find homeostasis after a seizure was another story. It was not just a simple "shut off and reboot" situation. It felt like I was being violated from the inside out, something I wanted to avoid at all costs.

It was difficult to calm my nerves down. My heart was still racing over 120 and the palpitations were beginning to concern me too. At times the rhythm of my heart felt abnormal and I knew this meant a risk of developing serious complications. Much as it's not good to run a marathon for days straight, it wasn't great for my heart to be this elevated for this many days either. Upon awakening, it seemed like it had reset to a rate of about 60, but it shot up again as soon as I ate anything and remained high most of the day.

Etsuko told me she had bumped into the palliative care doctor who had said that our mother had twenty-four to forty-eight hours to live. That's what she said two days prior. I think it's impossible to say when it's time to go. Maybe she would still be alive in five days when I got out of quarantine. I could only hope.

My sisters said they hoped her last words to them weren't that they were being too loud.

"Maybe ask her to say something nice to you," I suggested.

Our mother was someone who was so careful with her words, very kind and thoughtful, so scolding was out of character. The last time she had really scolded me was when I was six years old and had been caught climbing the shelves in the pantry to steal cookies. Halfway up the pantry, with my legs straddled between opposite shelves and sprawled like a starfish, cookie stuffed in my mouth and a couple more crushed in my hands, and suspended between flour and boxes of seaweed, I heard, "Momo, dame dame!" *Bad bad*, she'd scolded, and took the cookies from my hands as I choked down the ones in my mouth. I scurried off quickly to avoid getting my bum smacked. Tim Tams, the brand of cookie I had stolen, are still, to my mind, worth the scolding.

*****

I grew up in a quiet suburb of Perth in a house on a dead-end street. There was a large neighborhood park with a playground within a few minutes walking distance. Our house was on a hill, which made for exciting scooter rides zooming down the steep slope. I was sent to a private all-girls Christian school a mile away, where I walked or rode my bike to school. It was a very strict education with unflattering uniforms that resembled potato sacks. My friend Joanna would joke, "At least nobody would want to rape us wearing these hideous outfits." They were fully equipped with regulation underwear and bloomers for sports. Girls were raised to be proper, polite ladies and most definitely asexual. Looking back,

I appreciated all the values the school taught me, as well as the gift of self-discipline, which served me well through the rest of my life. I could have done without the heavy dose of guilt and the attitude that there's only one righteous way to live life. I managed to shed a lot of that as I traveled further away from my roots. However, I cannot deny the good that I received from my education and the long-lasting friendships I have held dear from primary school. I wouldn't have learned the importance of friends at a young age otherwise.

During quarantine, I reconnected with many close friends. Although decades had passed and we hadn't been in touch consistently, the bonds we had created as young people contained a deep connection that was maintained even to this day.

One of my friends suggested I ask my sisters to set up a video chat in the room, so I could feel like I was there, just to be present and not even necessarily have to say anything. Too much talking was bothering our mom at that point. They set up my mother's phone camera as a close-up of her face, giving me a front-row seat to her labored breathing. It was too much, so they moved the camera to the corner of the room, for a wide view of everything. From my hotel room, I watched my sisters massage my mom and chant Buddhist mantras as they took turns resting and going for breaks. I found it surprisingly comforting to see them all together from my tiny phone screen; it almost felt like I was there. It wasn't the same as being there, but it would do.

Late in the afternoon, one of my sisters let out a scream while they were giving our mother a back rub.

"Are you OK?" Keiko asked.

"Ewww," Etsuko groaned. "I just touched poo." Both laughing, I watched a flurry of activity to get wipes and clean up the mess.

"I guess this is karma, she cleaned our butts, now it's time to clean hers," I offered.

My mother's understanding of karma came to her in her mid-thirties. Her parents weren't particularly religious, although her family was mostly Shinto, a Japanese indigenous religion rooted in nature. She grew up in the countryside through elementary school, her family was mostly farmers. Whenever we visited Japan, we ate clementines that continued to grow for generations. Her father had tried to start several businesses; my favorite was a tire shop where he hand-carved grooves into worn tires. Our mom was the older of two girls to my grandmother, known as the town beauty with her large round eyes. My grandfather met my grandmother when she was twenty years old and fell in love with her on the spot. Seconds later, they were married and a year after, my mother was born. When my mother was in middle school, the family moved to Tokyo as my grandfather wanted to pursue a career in politics, which he achieved until his death in 1987. My mother wanted to become a dancer, but her father asked her to "not lift her legs up in public" as he was a public figure. She wanted to be respectful, so she ended up getting a degree in economics. She claimed she had no memory of anything that she studied, mostly because she spent four years of college playing golf, but also because she was not interested in the subject matter. She met my father in college and got married in 1972, after a few years of dating.

My grandfather wanted them to leave Japan because he was too influential and they wouldn't need to strive to be successful. They would inevitably get a free ride through life without having to prove themselves. My grandfather wanted his children to become proficient in English. He felt that knowing only Japanese was too limiting for their future. So, my parents were shipped off to Australia. I don't remember why they chose Australia, but my sense was that my grandfather probably wanted political connections. My mother's sister and her husband moved to Canada.

There was often quite a lot of political drama that happened as my grandfather climbed the ranks through the government. A local journalist published untruthful stories about my grandfather wanting to use Australia as a nuclear dumping ground. Journalists, like today, were free to blatantly lie behind a facade of accepted racism. Our house was egged, spray-painted with hate words, and my parents endured the stress of racism on a regular basis. With time it got better, as Australia became a more multicultural country.

My mother discovered Zen Buddhism when I was about twelve years old. She was searching for meaning after she had separated from my father, unable to make sense of how her marriage had come to an end. Divorce was still unacceptable in the Japanese culture and looked upon with shame. She was looking for a deeper understanding of life, seeking answers to questions about why certain things happen and what it all meant. Prior to Zen, she had dabbled in yoga, other Eastern philosophies, and crystals, to name a few religious and spiritual interests. There was a phase when there was a new spiritual path every month.

I could tell when she found Buddhism, it was more meaningful and potentially longer lasting, judging by her enthusiasm for it. She told me, for many years, she had been angry about her divorce, but her new religion had helped her to put the pain behind her. I was glad that she found something that gave her peace. Throughout the rest of her life, she continued to study Buddhism, meditated daily (sometimes for hours), and chanted mantras. She devoted endless hours to charitable work and encouraged her kids to think more about preparing ourselves for a better afterlife. I was barely making ends meet in the here and now, so I didn't have any reserves left to invest in my next life. I did my best not to be a douchebag, but according to my mother, that wasn't enough. She was concerned about the bad karma I was amassing.

Regrettably, I never had the opportunity to ask her specifically what bad karma I could expect for my next life. Maybe all the cookies would be stolen from me in my childhood, or my own children would paint my house with their snot. Interesting to note, my cat Zuko had a sinus infection for a year, and despite constant medical attention, blew yellow snot all over my house, and thanks to my mast cell disorder, I couldn't touch cookies.

Otherwise, I didn't get the concept of karma. We were, after all, talking about an invisible bank account of sorts—somewhere in another dimension, someone was taking notes of all the bad things I had been doing and keeping track of deposits and withdrawals from my karmic account. Took sister's pen—check. Stepped on an ant—check. Did this mean in the cosmic righting system that I'd be born as an ant and crushed by a giant pen? But how about the time when I helped the old lady cross the street? Does my ant-grandmother save me from getting squashed by the giant pen? My mother would say it's not that simple, but to me, it just sounded confusing.

One year, I didn't know what was worth abstaining from for Lent since I wasn't eating any of the unacceptable foods, so I gave up karma permanently instead. There were many years in my childhood that it seemed like extended Lent, as my mother explored some extreme diets. At one point, we only ate vegetables grown in our organic garden, which was often a magnet for bugs. To this day, I cannot eat broccoli without examining it thoroughly for worms. My complicated relationship with food first grew roots at a young age.

I had hoped that my mother would remarry or at least find a boyfriend, but that never transpired. There were some suitors, but she wasn't interested in compromising her freedom, and she remained single for her remaining decades. She didn't seem lonely. In fact, she seemed content, but every ten years or so, I'd ask her if she had any interest in finding a relationship. The last time we talked about it was a few years ago. She said, "I do think about it occasionally, that it would be nice to be with someone, but then the thought is quickly replaced by something else."

She seemed happy devoting her life to building meditation centers to share her teachings of Buddhism. She had hoped that I would follow in her footsteps, but I didn't, or couldn't. Chanting mantras was of crucial importance to her and she knew my attention span for learning mantras was that of a goldfish. She'd still try to teach me occasionally and gave up after I'd say mantras backwards, mixing them up with nursery rhymes. She often stopped me mid-mantra because I had unwittingly prayed to be turned into a donkey. She would laugh, saying that I was exhausting as her efforts to show me a more righteous life had failed. I just didn't "get it." And just as much as I didn't understand her path, although I respected it, she didn't understand my path either; my strong passion for being of service in the field of medicine.

Over the years, we learned how to adapt and how to connect, and as time passed, she made a greater effort to connect with me in genuine ways and let go of religious conversion. This was such a huge life lesson for me, how to foster love and nurture a connection with someone where there were so many fundamental disagreements in our approaches to life. Judging by my mother's actions, she saw the value in bridging this gap and found ways to communicate with me. I've seen other families divided by religion, politics, and other beliefs, but my mother knew better, and she taught me through her behavior that our differences could be set aside.

What my mother helped me to overcome is one of the biggest struggles, in my opinion, that we as humans are faced with: tribalism. How can we still love others when we do not agree? How can we accept others when our beliefs are different?

What an honor it was to have shared this incredible journey on our planet with this remarkable person. With love, we overcame our differences. My mother reached out with the olive branch and I accepted. World peace starts in our homes, and my mother not only provided that for me, but through her behavior, showed me how to practice patience and acceptance of those with beliefs I didn't share. We were united by our moral code. She taught me how to love without needing to agree with someone, and that love can exist, even if I don't like them or an idea they possess. My mother and I had conversations where she would say, "I know you don't like it when

I talk about things from a religious perspective." And I would respond, "But I want to know your opinion."

I listened and she didn't have the need to make her beliefs mine.

With mixed feelings of gratitude for my mother and deep sadness, I watched through my computer screen as her breath grew more and more shallow, and by the early evening, the death rattle started to settle in. The nurse said that they could give her medication to stop the frightening sound. She explained that it doesn't bother the patient, it's more for the family members. My sisters decided they didn't want her to have any more unnecessary medication and decided to go to sleep around 9 p.m. I suggested we could all video again the next day.

"I hope she will still be with us," Etsuko said.

I thanked my sisters for being with our mother and hoped I could see her again.

DAY TEN

The phone rang at 1:10 a.m. and I bolted upright with my heart pounding. I knew why I was getting the call. My mother had just passed. I was too tired to feel much, mostly numb. I tried to stay focused as we spent the next two hours on a video chat. I sat up, reclined in bed with my phone propped up against my bent knees.

My sisters recounted what had happened over the last few hours. We had all fallen asleep around the same time. Around 10 p.m., the nurse came into the room and said that she was no longer responsive. Etsuko felt her hand and reassured her that she was there. She laid back down and told our mom that she was just going to close her eyes, but that she was in the room. Etsuko fell back to sleep and woke up with a jolt around 12:45 a.m. as our mother let out a loud gasp of air. My sister sat up and held her hand. It was still warm. She had stopped breathing.

She called in the nurse to confirm that she had passed. That particular nurse wasn't sure and asked another nurse to come in. Our mother's face looked serene and the mild swelling in her face from kidney failure had smoothed out her wrinkles making her skin look very youthful, definitely not that of a seventy-two-year-old.

My sisters were noticeably upset that they weren't awake the moment she passed. We had all missed it. Many people pass in their sleep or alone; maybe this is their preference. Regardless, she knew we were very close by. We took our time to look at our mom's face and to say our goodbyes. I couldn't conjure up the energy to cry. I was lost for words.

At 4 a.m., I finally fell back asleep for a few hours.

*****

I woke up feeling heavy, metaphorically and physically. I still had four full days of hell to get through. I knew eating anything in this state would be a potential problem, but not eating was a problem too. I ate one bite of rice. I had a mild reaction, but it wasn't bad. I waited twenty minutes before I had another bite. I waited another twenty minutes and had another bite. For breakfast, I ate about four tablespoons of rice. At least I got something down. I wished that I didn't have to deal with eating at all. It felt overwhelming to deal with the shock of my mother passing while trying to figure out how to keep myself alive.

The numbness started to wear off as loss and sadness tagged in. It was too much pain and I didn't have the bandwidth to handle all my feelings. The hole I found myself in was dark and lonely. Just a little crying started to clog up my sinuses and ears, which were already vastly inflamed. Crying more would close up my sinuses and throat, and I was already struggling with breathing, so it wasn't the right time to open the floodgates and allow myself to cry without inhibition. I needed to quickly climb out onto steadier ground in order to shift my energy and mood and to avoid an emotionally induced physical collapse. I tried some Qigong; it wasn't enough. I tried some yoga, but bending forward made my sinus blockage worse. I tried meditation, but I was too agitated. Deep breathing wasn't working either. Watching any screen gave me a headache and it required too much energy to talk to anyone.

Then I heard a little voice in my mind say, "Dance."

I don't know where I found the energy. There must have been a little pocket of reserves tucked away waiting for this moment. I put on some music that I thought my mom would like, and I danced in ceremony, surrounded in my mind's eye by all my ancestors who had passed. I rejoiced at the reunion of her soul with my father, her parents, as well as all our pets that we had loved. There were a few tears of joy that she had crossed over and I celebrated her return to the world of spirits. It was a dance to celebrate her life. Although alone in my room, I sensed my mom was close by and saying, "Ganbatte," *do your best*, and I promised everyone in the spirit world that I would give life my best shot. Dancing always made me feel happy. It didn't matter if I had just been dumped, or if I was going through something awful, I knew that in the hour or so in a dance class, everything was perfect in the moment, a respite from my reality. I felt joy spread throughout my body and flood my mind as I allowed myself to enjoy the natural high of the endorphins until—

OH MY GOD, CALF CRAMP!

I was taken out of my bliss. I had used up my morsel of stored energy. I collapsed and became a jiggling jellyfish on the carpet.

There was one small regret that I had had with my father before he passed. He had asked me to dance with him at my sister's wedding, and I said no because I was too shy. To this day, it's just one of those things. It's so small, but I've always regretted that decision, and out of all the things that I feel like I missed out on in life, that was it. All things considered, it's pretty fortunate to live with such little regret. I promised myself I would take more risks when opportunities presented themselves, especially if I was feeling shy or nervous. I didn't want to miss another dance. My father passed away a few years after my sister's wedding, but over the next few years, due largely to the distance, I only saw him three more times before he died. We never know when someone will be taken from our lives and I remind myself to take all the given opportunities to accept a dance and to express gratitude to everyone in my life.

*****

As my first day on Earth without my mom progressed, I found myself having conversations with her in my mind. I wanted to believe that she communicated with me somehow and that she was OK.

"Mom? How is it on the other side?" I asked in my mind, visualizing her freely floating around the planet.

"It's spectacular!" I imagined her saying.

"Is Dad there? How about Grandma?" I continued.

"Everyone is here," I heard her voice in my mind. "Even my cat."

I felt happy for the first time since entering quarantine. "I hope to see you and everyone else soon," I responded.

"You still have about thirty years left," my mother said in a matter-of-fact tone. I had no idea how she knew that, but I was comforted that I'd probably make it out of quarantine alive.

"What can you tell me about your life?" I asked.

"There was a lot of screaming and jumping up and down, then it ended." She laughed.

I was glad that my mother had retained her sense of humor even in the afterlife.

I was in total acceptance that this perceived communication with my mother might have been completely fabricated by my mind, but it did offer me some comfort to dwell in these delusions. Late-onset schizophrenia aside, it made me feel connected to her. Nobody can say what will happen after the great mystery of death. Those who claim they have returned back to earth from having a near-death experience—although possibly valid and not meaning to dismiss their experience—could just be hallucinating. However, I wanted to keep an open mind to the possibility of existence in the afterlife. I had made my mother vow that we would see each other again, so I was holding her to this promise!

I wanted to embrace all the beautiful qualities and be a living example of the moral code that my mother lived by. Life isn't supposed to be perfect. Don't expect good things to happen all the time, that's just not realistic. As a family, we may fight at times and that's perfect the way it is. We need to occasionally let off steam with family because we can't let it out in public. Sometimes we just need some space, because we all drive each other crazy. You make a mistake, you say sorry, no big deal. If you are together in public and someone acts poorly, pretend you're not related to them. A little more about that later.

A trait of a good Japanese mother, possibly all mothers, seems to be endless worrying. I often found myself sugar-coating things for my mom because I was concerned she might worry too much. I told her, "Don't worry." She would joke, "I'll try, but I'll worry nonetheless."

Maybe it was the way she expressed love. It's a very Japanese way to communicate love and I grew to appreciate it more as I got older. When I was younger, I found myself getting irritated by her over-worrying. "I'm just fine, stop worrying so much!" However, I evolved. As my tits sagged more and more, so did my appreciation for her concern. I wondered what my mother would be worrying about now, her spirit hovering above the earthly plane. I imagined her looking down at me with her kind eyes, at her eldest daughter, barely coping, highly dysfunctional, and thinking, "She'll be fine, and if not, I'll see her sooner than planned."

Lost in my despair during my visit to her, I had forgotten to say the most important things. I closed my eyes and visualized her sitting in the chair in front of me. I held her hand and said to her, "Thank you for being such a good mom."

DAY ELEVEN

As I was processing my grief of losing my mother, I was simultaneously grieving the loss of being able to eat. In the past, like with any loss, I went through all the stages of grieving too. There were times when I got angry at my own body and just told it needed to deal with whatever I gave it. "Mind over matter." "Brain over grain."

This could go on for months, thinking this was just a temporary thing that would correct itself the next day. The denial cost me a heavy investment in toilet paper and a sore bum. Even now, I still get caught in denial and think I can just have a bite of something that I can't eat. Under stressful situations, most people either lose their appetite or it increases significantly. Very few people eat normally. My appetite wasn't affected. I was starving, but I couldn't eat anything. Just a bite of anything made my face tingly and numb, my sinuses started to close over, my heart rate doubled, and I got very dizzy from my blood pressure dropping quickly. I knew my body wasn't ready for any food yet. I imagined when I was an infant and thought I lost my mother permanently, being left hungry for long periods; it probably felt similar to what I felt now. I couldn't have had the cognitive awareness, but maybe the feelings were the same. I was lost in despair, my heart was crushed, and I was starving.

During my MA program in psychology, my professor said that the process of grief is about completion. Those who don't have much to process may not have much of a grieving path. What he referred to as completion were the unprocessed emotions that we still had about the deceased and what unfulfilled dreams we still had with that person. Letting go of all the feelings, as well as the hopes for the future, make up all the different stages of grief. Having an intellectual understanding of this may help on some level, but going through it is another story. Sometimes getting too brainy about it may actually deter grief and prolong healing.

As I mentioned, intellectualization is a defense mechanism that allows you to minimize feelings or even avoid them all together. Hiding in the ivory tower of my mind wouldn't heal my pain. Grief, much like life, is highly unpredictable in terms of when the stages may hit. My best friend, who passed away, was only forty-one, leaving two young children behind. It was such a painful experience for everyone. I myself spent the first two years in shock, not processing much of the loss, but then I went through the bulk of my grief two years later, when I cried hysterically for months on end. As for grieving my mother, I was sure it would be a unique journey. It would be whatever it needed to be.

My mother and I had planned a trip to Japan, which unfortunately had been postponed due to the pandemic. I had always been fascinated by ninja culture and we had planned to visit a ninja village—an actual theme park in Japan where ninja skills were taught. You'd get to explore the life of being a ninja.

As a child, I spent many years pretending to be a ninja, learning how to breathe underwater with a straw and jumping off rooftops, much to the concern of all adults around me. I still carried this curiosity until now and had been looking forward to going to the ninja museum. We had also planned to learn about the indigenous people of Japan, the Ainu. My father was from Hokkaido and I felt like we could be descendants of the Ainu as some of our physical features resembled them. If given the opportunity to travel to Japan, I'll travel there with my parents' memories. It won't be the same without my mother, and not having her with me would likely cause sadness, but I would travel with her spirit.

In retrospect, I began processing the death of my mother as soon as we had received her terminal diagnosis. Knowing she had little time left, I found the initial feelings I confronted were rooted in panic. I felt like I was skydiving without a parachute or a net to catch me. I felt like a part of me, or sometimes all of me was dying.

My worst panic attack occurred while I was driving home from work one day. The air was thick with pollen and my lungs were irritated. My mother had declined treatment and I was having difficulty wrapping my mind around the current circumstances. As I drove onto the highway, I felt out of control, my breathing started to become rapid, and I started to feel nauseous. Was I going to pass out, throw up, and crash my car? I called a friend to help me calm down. Finally, I was able to get home.

Unfortunately, these panic attacks continued several times per week. I didn't want to try a new medication because I was concerned about the side effects; they tend to give me more side effects than symptom relief. I tried some CBD oil, which seemed to take off the edge. I expressed my fears to my friends about the feeling that I was flailing through space unprotected and they convinced me that they would be my safety net. They were my chosen family.

Everything that transpired in the hotel made me question if I should have bolted back off the plane at JFK to avoid all this heartache and pain alone. However, there was some serendipity or grace that might have played into allowing me to get back to Perth in time. I discovered that the flights from Singapore to Perth the day after I arrived were mostly canceled or rerouted to Brisbane. If I had left a day later, I would have needed to quarantine in Brisbane or another city and would not have had the thirty-minute visit with my mother. I wished I had left a week earlier. My mother had still been going out for meals with her friends and was quite mobile then. There was no way we could have known her death would sneak up on us this abruptly.

We were able to talk on the phone regularly and it just didn't seem that urgent. For many weeks, I didn't know how I would be able to handle the quarantine process. My hesitation had caused me to be stuck in isolation dealing with the greatest loss that I had ever experienced. I had passively waited until I knew I had to go, but it seemed like I should have taken a more active role in choosing. It's almost a pity that I didn't care more about the validation of others, as I would have pushed myself to leave earlier. I had gotten stuck, wedged between seeking approval from others and my own fears of quarantine. In the end, I didn't move fast enough.

Do we have much choice in when it's our time to go? Can we put an X on the calendar and mark our expiration date? Does the Grim Reaper put us into his schedule and come down at the last second to take our spirit? Or does he sit around, twiddling his thumbs, playing Sudoku, glancing over every so often to check if our time is up? And how much does "will" play into our life expectancy? Do we stay around longer because we want to, or does the body machine start to terminate independently of what the mind wants?

All these questions swam around my mind without any right or wrong answers, but it seemed necessary to at least ask them. I gave myself a headache overthinking the incomprehensible. Finally, I opted to watch kitten rescue videos instead.

DAY TWELVE

For breakfast, they served a salad. Vegetables, finally, but for breakfast?! Guests posted, "What the hell was up with the salad?" Reportedly it wasn't a bad salad, but who serves Cobb salad at 6 a.m.? And when did they make this salad? Unlikely at 4 a.m. It was probably days old. The staff admitted to a mix up, they had served lunch for breakfast, so dinner would be for lunch. Did that mean dinner would be stale pancakes with cereal?

For me, more quinoa and not-moldy green beans. I changed how I prepared my meals. Sometimes the green beans were in larger chunks, other times, they were smaller. Green beans on the side of the quinoa. Quinoa mixed with green beans. Served cold, warm, or hot. I got really creative with my meal that morning and made a circle of quinoa and a smiley face with the green beans. I looked at my happy meal and realized I wasn't happy at all. I stabbed out the eyes first, ate them, and as a silent tear rolled down my cheek, I rearranged the beans to make a sad face.

There were two more days left until I could be released. I was in the home stretch now. The phone rang and it was the medical team checking in and letting me know they would be stopping by for the fourth and final COVID test during quarantine. "Any symptoms?" they asked.

"No, I'm OK." I lied. It was too much to go into everything in detail and I didn't have the energy to even talk. The truth was that my nose had been running on and off all morning, but it was sadness dripping out of my nostrils, unrelated to COVID. And, of course, I couldn't smell anything; my nose was out of commission thanks to the histamine overload still coursing through my system.

Fatigue? Yes, that too! There's something so emotionally exhausting about grieving, it feels like I'd bottomed out and couldn't hold onto any energy. I tried not to cry too much either, as my tear factory workers needed a vacation too. I needed to shut down temporarily to get my head above ground, as I felt like I had been too immersed in loss, and I needed to come up for air.

Numbness, to me, is a bit of an emotional vacation, a little reprieve from the tsunami of emotions that had hit me hard during the last two months. I recognized there were probably a lot of feelings to process about my mom's passing, but the quiet after the storm felt like a crack had opened in the bolted window, and a whiff of fresh air had whooshed in through my soul. I think I had been breathing so shallowly by default since entering quarantine I forgot that half my lungs existed.

Maybe it was the sky clearing after the last few days that had been so overcast and surly that contributed to my clearer mind and calmer mood. Whatever it was, I welcomed it. Considering everything I had gone through, it was going to be a matter of time before whatever I had swept under the rug over the past few months would be rearing its three-headed, monstrous ugliness and spewing out its innards.

Very generally speaking, whenever we have a significant emotional reaction, but can't process it fully in the moment, it gets stored. I'm not talking about getting pissed off after missing the bus, but about things that hold more weight. Those stored emotions take energy for us to keep down as we try to get on with our lives. At some point, the balance starts to tip where the feelings we stuff down outweigh the energy we have to keep our conscious mind clear, and overspill occurs.

But right then, I still had enough conscious energy to keep my feelings at bay. My defense mechanisms were still intact. There's no need to go looking for this potential shitshow now. I didn't need to shove my fist up my own ass, digging for crap. It would come looking for me all in due time.

The day rolled by. The funeral home was chosen and I told my sisters to pick whichever coffin they wanted. Everything about the funeral felt too triggering to talk about. I was only half listening to the conversations to protect myself from any unwanted emotional overreactions. But coffins aren't cheap. I suddenly blurted out, "When it's time for me to go, can you just order the cardboard version for me?"

As I wouldn't be getting out of quarantine for a few more days, my sisters asked if I wanted to postpone the funeral until then. I wanted to be supportive of my family by being present, but wasn't sure whether seeing my mother in the coffin would cause unnecessary trauma or if the closure would be a good thing. The funeral home was quite busy, so the viewing ended up being scheduled for a week after her death. I would see my mother one last time. At least it would give me a few days to recuperate between getting out of quarantine and attending the funeral. I hoped that I would be on steadier ground by then.

I didn't want to provoke another emotional upheaval, so I watched TV bloopers and stand-up comedy. I avoided talking to all my friends. Everyone was so supportive and kind, but just being asked, "How are you?" was an invitation to open the floodgates. I couldn't take the risk of an emotional eruption, as my sinuses were open just by a sliver, and I was tired through my marrow. My tank was empty and what lay behind a thin veneer, barely keeping me together, was a messy conglomeration that frightened me.

DAY THIRTEEN

My last full day in quarantine and the little mental vacation from yesterday was over. My body felt like lead, and after twelve hours of being relatively motionless in the spongy bed, I thought it was probably best to overcome inertia and get up. My legs felt weak and my eyes had trouble focusing. I hobbled over to my bitchen to make something to eat. The lack of proper nutrition meant that I was mostly going into my reserves for energy, which were already limited. My stomach churned without enough food as the acid ate away at my insides. The low blood sugar made me feel irritable and jumpy like my nerves were on the outside surface of my skin. I was so uncomfortable that I wanted to crawl out of myself. This was compounded by being confined inside four walls. I felt like a pressure cooker at maximum capacity. My feelings, the pain, and the trauma, were all about to spill over.

For me, healing meant allowing myself to feel the full range of emotions that had been stuffed down in the moment, because it was impossible to deal with the tragic nature of the actual situation. I knew there would come a time when I couldn't continue to say, "Later feelings, I'll get to you when I have time." I would have appreciated manageable and appealing hors d'oeuvres-sized portions to be digested at a convenient time. Of course, that doesn't typically happen, as the pressurized emotional system builds while we try to get on with our lives, and when we least expect it, we hit our tipping point. Then BAM! there's no more holding it back. At this point, we can deal with the volcanic emotional eruption and start to clean up. There's also an option not to deal with it, but then you're sitting around in your own, stinky trash pile. There's not much middle ground.

I started part of this emotional purge on day thirteen of my quarantine. *Why couldn't my mom wait four days to die? And why did she have to fall? If she hadn't fallen, she would have been able to avoid all those harsh medications that probably sped up her death.* I'd flown halfway around the world and endured hell and torture in quarantine to see her for thirty minutes, which I think I could have done without.

How I wished my last memory of her could have been the one from January 1, 2020, when she warmly hugged me goodbye outside her apartment when one of my high school besties picked me up to go to the airport. It was a perfectly warm evening, and the smell of the magnolia tree that stood magnificently outside my mother's building saturated the air. I should have settled on that last memory. It all just didn't seem worth what I went through.

I didn't want to feel angry at my mom because, obviously, it wasn't her fault, but I felt at least a bit miffed that she couldn't hang in for just a few extra days. Why had life allowed this to happen? I recognized I wasn't alone, so many had lost family members during the pandemic and couldn't hold their mothers' hands too. It seemed so inhumane and lacking dignity. And what in the damned hell was up with the delivery of moldy green beans? What incompetent half-wit thinks it's OK to sell compost as fresh groceries?

And while I was at it, why wasn't my mother's will not strong enough to live an extra week? Was I not important enough for her to want to see me? What did I get out of all of this other than saving a few bucks by not eating anything? Was this all just a cruel lesson to show me that I should have listened to my instincts? That coming to Perth was a horrid idea? Where was my personal Jesus to answer these questions? Definitely not in room 2025 at the Pan Pacific.

I stumbled around in my mind to find answers. Maybe my mother was actually angry at me for something. That I had moved halfway around the world. That I had left my coat on the floor. Maybe this was her final screw you to me. I'll never know, I guess if she had held a lifetime's worth of resentment towards me. I'm sure I pissed her off regularly when I was a snotty and obstinate child and definitely when I was a rebellious and annoying teenager. Finally, what was I supposed to do with all these thoughts? Send a letter to the Better Brahman Bureau and complain?

Dear   Supreme   Existence,   Absolute
Reality,   or   whatever   you   respectfully
refer to yourself as,

WTF?

Metaphorically yours,

Momoko

The frustration I felt towards the health department for taking so long to get my exemption had steam coming out of my ears. If I had gotten out two days before, I might have been able to have a conversation with her. Did they intentionally make it unnecessarily difficult in order to prevent people from getting out of quarantine? I understood that they wanted to protect the public, but at the expense of traumatizing so many individuals? There must have been a better way to handle this situation with greater compassion while still keeping the masses safe. I felt a level of disdain for the government and how they had prevented families from being together at the most crucial times in their lives.

As the last night of quarantine approached, tired from all the mental gymnastics, the conclusion I drew was that my mother's passing was randomly timed. There was no way I could have predicted what I would endure. It was like getting hit by an ice cream truck that materialized out of nowhere. I couldn't have seen any of this coming, there were no warning signs. If anything, the signs pointed in the opposite direction. It was misleading, like a sign over the George Washington Bridge from New York to New Jersey welcoming me to the Bahamas.

So much of life is random, and my mind doesn't handle nonlinear events well; it prefers reasons and answers to questions, as that's much easier to categorize experiences and file them away. But I needed to find closure to the inexplicable. I feared what had been swept under the rug. I didn't even want to lift the corner to what might be down there, but I could feel the inner stirrings, the rumblings of quakes from deep within.

DAY FOURTEEN

I can't say I was excited to get out of hotel quarantine. Although, I definitely wasn't sad about leaving either. Stories circulated about the many people who had been psychologically damaged for the long term upon being released from quarantine, which made me weary, especially with my health challenges, my mom passing, and the experience of claustrophobia. I wondered how I would fare in the free world. What would my re-entry back into life be like? Would I join the statistic of people who developed post-traumatic stress disorder, and each time a door closed me inside a room, would my heart start to race? Would I have fitful nights of sleep riddled with nightmares about being attacked and suffocated by giant green bean monsters? Only time would tell the extent of the trauma that has been caused. I hoped that I had protected my mind and heart as much as possible so that this dreadful experience wouldn't plague me forever.

I got a quick glimpse into my fractured mind when I found myself getting stuck in a looming thought: How would I feel about staying at my mom's house? Would it be creepy? Maybe her ghost would stalk me around her house, and she would somehow torment me. As my mind filtered through paranormal paranoia, I freaked myself out enough to stop packing my bags and ponder what I would do if I saw my mother's ghost materialize in front of me. Would she cast evil spells onto me and show up as a floating decapitated head in a ring of spitting fire? Or maybe she'd jump out of the closet in the middle of the night.

Then I laughed at myself. I could imagine my father's spirit doing this, but not my mother's. Totally up his alley. My mother, on the other hand, was more likely to hang out in the laundry room and remind me not to wash my wool sweaters in high temperatures. Before I even got out of quarantine, I had manifested some significant delusional thinking as my rational mind lost the battle against insanity.

There was an extra knock at my door shortly after the breakfast knock. I opened the door to find my hotel-quarantine-release paperwork. The letter stated I would be able to leave at 2:16 p.m. Not 2:15 p.m....2:16 p.m. We Australians are a precise bunch.

11:16 a.m.: The nurse called and asked me if I had any COVID-related symptoms. I actually had a runny nose, congestion, fatigue, and a headache, but I lied again. The health department needed to figure out a better way of asking questions. Admitting these symptoms would have resulted in more tests and an unbearable prolonging of my stay. It threatened to become a Groundhog Day of eternal testing as these symptoms weren't going away anytime soon. I was informed that my jail break had been moved up to 1:54 p.m.

I made my last meal: no surprises, quinoa and green beans. There was no pleasure left in eating at this point. I ate to survive— it was fuel. I had probably dropped 10 lb. during quarantine and I had been underweight to start, so my body was converting energy from my muscles. A suboptimal situation. I had a strategy to put on weight after I got home, but for now, I just needed to be able to function to get through the rest of my stay in Australia without losing any more weight or my mind. The plan was a high-calorie diet, rich in protein, with strength training to rebuild muscle. Much like the last year of the pandemic, with very little room for strategizing, I wondered how my plan would pan out. I seasoned my fuel with sprinkles of sea salt and munched away, grateful that I had made it this far alive and without a visit to the ER. Still, I didn't have spare calories at the moment other than those necessary to just get through the day. And now that I was anticipating the arrival of my parents' ghosts and what that said about my fragile sanity, I was going to need enough calories to equal several cheeseburgers and milkshakes to help restore balance and sense. When I was in elementary school, my mother often took me to a diner at our local shopping mall, where I discovered spearmint milkshakes. A milkshake would probably kill me right now, but I closed my eyes and imagined myself sitting at the diner with my mom, sipping on a light-green, thick, creamy milkshake. I felt a tiny bit better.

At exactly 1:54 p.m. I opened my door and I peered out.

Within seconds, every hallway door opened and the inmates stood in a single file. Some chatted casually as if nothing had happened. I was half expecting, or maybe hoping, that a bunch of deranged people who looked like they'd stuck their fingers in electric sockets would emerge. But to my disappointment, everyone looked like they'd kept up with proper hygiene and acted as if it were just another day. At least they looked like they had weathered the terms of the quarantine well, from the outside, anyway. I guessed I probably looked the same to them too, but I felt pretty beaten-up and bruised internally. The prospect of launching out of quarantine and into cleaning up my mother's house seemed harrowing at best. I wasn't sure if I'd feel like I'd walked into a haunted house or just be stung by the emptiness of her not being there. Regardless, it felt like I was still raw from everything that had transpired and I would not only be rubbing salt into the wound but maybe some cayenne pepper as well.

I looked around to see if I could spot the woman in tears who had struggled with her suitcase two weeks ago, but she wasn't there. I wondered if she had been the one who'd come down with the coronavirus or if she'd experienced another medical issue and been transferred to the hospital. Maybe she'd made a run for it. That's what I hoped was true.

We stood in the corridor with our bags for about five minutes before they started allowing people to leave. I was about the tenth person in line and there were around the same number of people behind me. We were instructed to socially distance ourselves.

I felt a little dizzy standing. I sensed my blood pressure was probably low, my ears and sinuses were clogged. I was anxious for many reasons, my stomach was uncomfortable, and I felt very tired. I clumsily pushed my two suitcases and three bags down the corridor—they felt a lot heavier than when I checked in. I showed my paperwork to the guard by the elevator, who checked the name in my passport against my paperwork, shuffled them together, and handed them back to me. Another guard stood by the elevator to direct people and pushed the lobby button. Only one guest entered an elevator, despite the fact that everyone was COVID-free. Wasn't that the whole purpose of quarantine? None of this made any sense, but who cares, I was getting out of there. My elevator made an extra stop on the eleventh floor and a young guy stood in front of the open door. He looked puzzled, I waved hi to him and the guard standing next to him yelled at the young guy, "Don't get in!" as one of his feet hovered over the threshold. He retreated quickly and the doors closed. When they next opened, I found myself in the lobby.

I had to show my passport with the paperwork again as I got off the elevator. I'm not sure what shenanigans people have gotten up to in the past, but I doubt there's much margin of error between getting onto an elevator and getting off it. I handed the guard my paperwork and passport, no chit-chat, just a nod as I followed a guy who must have come from another floor. He was carrying a very large surfboard, which I'm sure came in handy in a small hotel room. Maybe this was his chosen hobby for two weeks—indoor surfing.

At least the surfboard made it easy to socially distance. Subtle shifts of the surfer's body cleared out impressive space around him. The third guard, as I was about to leave the hotel, looked at my passport and paperwork again. She asked me to pay my bill, but I explained that I had paid over the phone. She said that wasn't possible, and that the hotel doesn't process payments over the phone. I rolled my eyes as wide open as I could since my mask covered all my other facial expressions. My patience was pretty thin, but I managed to bite my tongue and stopped myself from blurting out, "Oh my god, how long have you been working here and don't know about express check-out over the phone?"

But the polite Asian in me took over, which was smart since my freedom was only twelve feet away. She asked me again to pay. I flagged down someone standing in the concierge to check if I had paid. She came over with a clipboard and told guard number three that I had prepaid, to which she replied, "Oh, you really paid?" I wanted to flip the guard the bird, but I said thank you, instead, and walked out the front door.

A group of young women gaggled closely without masks and wearing slip-and-fall, high-risk, four-inch heels, they waltzed into the hotel to the ritzy bar in the lobby. They giggled in that youthful twenties way that you can only do when your brain isn't fully formed yet. I wanted to warn them about the coronavirus cases on the eleventh floor. *You should be wearing masks as well as skirts under your oversized belts.* I was in a horrible mood. They all looked amazing, and I looked like I was on a jailbreak mission in sneakers and an oversized hoodie that could house three pregnant women.

I stepped out of the hotel and waited at the main entrance for Keiko to pick me up. It was a perfect autumn day—a cool fresh breeze with a comforting sun. And I was free.

My claustrophobia melted away and the thought of having a challenging transition to too much freedom was quickly forgotten. I was the only person still wearing my mask. It was like my security blanket behind which I was hiding my traumatic two-week experience.

My sister arrived and gave me a warm hug as she welcomed me back home.

"We don't have mask mandates as of today, so you're welcome to take it off." She kindly informed me.

"I feel naked when I take it off, like I'm walking around without pants on," I said, but took off my mask anyway. I felt the gentle wind caress my cheeks and was glad I did.

"How are you?" she asked.

"Terrible." I didn't feel the need to sugarcoat anything. "It was total hell. And I don't recommend it for anyone. It's crazy-making, and unless you absolutely need to do it, just stay at home." Losing your mother is bad enough. Losing your mother in quarantine is the worst.

It wasn't a situation where, at the moment, there was a silver lining. The takeaway was that I felt tested and I barely made it. Maybe it had made me more resilient, but I didn't really think I needed more resilience. I was already donning fifteenth-century full body armor with a shield and now I had acquired a bulletproof vest and face guard to put over it. In my opinion, there's a point where there's just too much resilience. I hate the saying, "What doesn't kill you, makes you stronger." It almost killed me, I barely survived, and I didn't feel stronger—I felt very weak.

I asked Keiko how she was coping. "It's so sad, but I'm OK," she replied, explaining that she felt like she had done everything she could for our mom. She had helped take care of our mother and was present for almost all her doctor appointments, which was not an easy task working full-time and being a mother. She expressed that she didn't have any regrets and she hoped that I didn't either. I was happy for her that she felt this way, but we were evidently at very different places in our grieving. It didn't seem like the appropriate time to unleash where things stood for me, so I let the conversation morph into another direction.

Having my sister with me as we entered our mother's house was a welcomed distraction. We opened the door and for a fleeting moment, I thought that this had all been a bad dream and that our mom would greet us there as she had in the past. I felt a little dagger in my heart as I woke up from my altered state.

I often experienced walking into people's homes as a deeper view into their personas, a journey through their auras. I experienced being in someone's home like an intensified conversation about who they are and a glimpse into how they lived their lives. My fear that I would be confronted by a sense of ghostly eeriness dissipated quickly as I recognized that her house didn't feel empty. It still felt like her, and I was comforted by being in the peace she had cultivated in her home. She had infused her calm spirit into each room. In a way, she was still there, and if the walls could speak, they would speak of serenity, simplicity, and beauty.

"Your hair looks like Einstein's hair but without the genius part," I could almost hear my mother say.

Except these walls were quiet today about my appearance.

During the daylight, being in my mother's house felt calm, but as night fell and my sister returned home, my imagination got the better of me. I found myself feeling quite afraid. I don't think my mother's spirit would in any way want to intimidate me, but my overactive mind wasn't doing me any favors. I had nightmares for several nights and found myself waking up in a sweat and sitting bolt upright in bed with palpitations. It's just a bad dream, I told myself while I tried to bring down my heart rate. I had dreams in which I was stabbed to death, buried in a coffin alive, chased by demonic beings, driving without functioning brakes, crashing the car, and killing myself. I also had more benign dreams, like being in public without my underpants on, naked from the waist down. After about five nights, I recognized that my parents weren't psycho killers when they were alive and likely hadn't randomly become sociopathic in death. My nightmares diffused and my fractured mind started to sew itself up—it was holding itself together by a single thread.

RETURNING HOME

I ended up staying almost two weeks to pack away my mother's life. It was a cathartic process and mostly healing. There was so much joy in unraveling all the unintentional gifts that she had left behind. She had kept some sentimental pieces from our childhood, things we had written, artwork, and random items that she thought would be meaningful to us as adults. Stamp collections from when I was ten years old, costume jewelry, and hundreds of photos neatly organized into albums. So many personal treasures and memories to cherish and moments to reflect on my relationship with my parents and my childhood. There were, of course, albums full of embarrassing moments: me at age two sitting on the swan potty grunting to take a poop; the hideous, period-red, velour prom dress with '80s high-bang hairdo; and poolside pictures of me in a completely see-through swimwear. I think my grandmother put most of these albums together, bless her blind soul.

Being immersed in my mother's belongings for a fortnight, the greatest gift I discovered was not a lost piece of jewelry but the realization of how much we were loved. Of course, I knew she loved us, but there was something so special about rediscovering her unique way of preserving the small things we had made and how she took great care to keep them for us. Nothing had monetary value, but rather something greater than money, the value of a mom who was so proud of our smallest achievements.

My mother was a jewelry designer and she owned a boutique for decades. When I was in college, I had the opportunity to work there part-time and created signs for the store. I was surprised to see that she kept a framed sign with the opening hours of her store that I had handwritten when I was sixteen, quite poorly, complete with erased pencil line indentations still visible at the right angle of light.

During my stay at my mother's, I encountered many of her neighbors. Although I felt like I should hurry to move on to the next task, something made me stay to take the time to chat with everyone. She had lived in the apartment building for almost twenty years. No one was particularly close from what I could gather, and my mother tended to keep to herself, but there was   caring and thoughtfulness. Everyone I met who knew my mother, not just neighbors, but friends and healthcare workers, consistently said two things: How fond they were of her and how special she was. Of course, she was one of the most unique people to me, but it wasn't just the fact that she was my mother; it was who she was as a person. I told my mother's neighbor that my goal was to be half as special as she was. Lately, I felt more "special needs" than anything, but my goal was to shoot for landing somewhere on the special spectrum. I'd be content if I ended up being half as extraordinary as my mom.

My mother, being the considerate person she was, didn't want anyone to attend her funeral. She didn't want anyone to feel obligated to go, to take time off from their busy lives for her. I think she didn't realize that others might have wanted to say goodbye. Her friends, my friends, and my sisters' friends who had known our mother from childhood would all want the opportunity to pay their respects to the departure of her beautiful spirit. She might not have thought that her kids would want the support of all of these people. She had been such a private and fiercely independent person, and towards the end of her life, she solely leaned on my sisters.

Her friends made it clear that they wanted to attend a funeral, and from what I gathered from her closest friend, in quite large numbers. I felt a bit mean telling my friends, "I'm so sorry, it's only family," when they had been part of my acquired family from as young as three. However, these were my mother's wishes, and we wanted to respect her. Western Australia restricted gatherings of over five hundred people, so we couldn't even use COVID as an excuse. My sadness grew as I mulled over my mother's self-perception as a burden.

I felt extremely anxious about seeing my mother at the funeral, even to the point of feeling nauseous thinking about it. Much like seeing her in person for the last time, I was again concerned that I'd literally lose my shit—the combination of my unsettled stomach and my nerves regarding the funeral. I convinced myself that I'd be OK since I'd attended many funerals and never pooped my pants. Keiko had asked me to bring my mother's prayer beads and a few religious items, which I carried in a small bag. I arrived at the funeral home before it opened and I paced around. I pressed my face into the window to see if anyone was there. Right at 9 a.m., the lights went on and the doors opened. I was greeted quietly by the attendant with a nod and ushered into the waiting room. The funeral home was no frills, but my mother wouldn't have wanted anything extravagant.

There were enough cookies to feed an army and a pitcher of water. While I was wondering how many other funerals the cookies had sat on the platter, my sister and her daughter in a pink dress walked in. I was wearing my mother's clothes, dressed in black. I played with the idea of showing up in a floral dress that my mother had bought me the last time I saw her. My conservative voice won the debate. The attendant showed us into the viewing room. Feeling a little sick and my tummy grumbling, I wondered about that literal lose-my-shit moment. I gave my sister the bag of my mom's things and quickly ran into the bathroom.

Nothing happened, not even a skid mark, so I chalked it up to anxiety. I walked out again into the viewing room, and I knew it was time to say goodbye to my mom. My throat felt so tight that I had difficulty swallowing. I tried to slow down my breathing as I started to feel a little panicky approaching the casket. I peered into the coffin with just one eye. Rather surprised at what I saw, I stuck my head squarely over the head of the casket and took a closer look. This didn't look like my mother at all. I wanted to tell the attendant that she had the wrong Asian lady. They surely had made a mistake! My mother told me that when I was born, she was heavily sedated and she barely remembered the birth. Back in the day, babies were immediately separated from their mothers and taken to the nurses' room to be evaluated. Many hours later, I was brought to my mother in her recovery room. My mother told me that I looked very different to her when she saw me for the second time. My eyes were swollen shut and bruised like I had been defeated in a boxing match. She told the nurse that this wasn't her baby. The nurse was very embarrassed and quickly took me back to the nursery, only to return about an hour later to tell my mother that this was indeed her baby, as there were no other Asian babies in the hospital.

This rejection at birth became a recurring theme throughout my life. Whenever I said anything unacceptable to my mother, she disowned me. My mother and I were riding a crowded subway. I was twelve and read Japanese at about a five-year-old level. I pointed at an ad informing her that mangos were on sale, but lost in translation and with poor pronunciation, I enthusiastically yelled out, "look, mom! Tasty vaginas are cheap!" My mother shook her head and informed others, "we aren't related."

This person I couldn't recognize in the casket had a swollen face. All the extra skin had been stretched out, then pinned to the side, an extra roll of it surrounding her face. The skin had been pulled too tautly and it flattened her face completely, giving her a military chin. The makeup, although not horrible, wasn't anything she would wear. The foundation did match well, though, which is something my mother never quite mastered when alive. Her face and neck were always different tones, but today they matched perfectly—probably not having a chin helped with the blended look. I was so distracted by my mother's appearance, along with the Spotify ads that played between each tranquil, zen flute song, as well as my sister reprimanding the attendant that they should have the paid version of Spotify, that I forgot to be sad for quite some time.

Four of my mother's close friends attended the viewing, two I had known from my childhood. It was good to see them despite the circumstances. We all had an opportunity to say our final goodbyes to my mother. My gut instincts that I didn't need to invest in adult diapers were true. The most dreaded part of the funeral was over.

The attendants closed the casket and reminded us that they wouldn't be opening it again at the crematorium. Keiko joked that maybe they switched the bodies so we wouldn't know who they were cremating. As far as we knew, they could have been running a side business of organ smuggling.

The crematorium had a basket of rosemary sprigs next to the

casket. "How do they know she liked rosemary? She used to eat a ton of it with lamb." I asked the attendant why the rosemary was there and she said it symbolized remembrance and we could place it on the casket. That made much more sense than lamb chop garnish. My sister, niece, and I surrounded the casket with rosemary. My niece made sure to stick every sprig into the floral arrangement as we remembered all those who had passed before us, as well as those who were not with us in person.

As our mother was committed into the crematorium, my niece said, "Grandma is really dead now." To my niece's point, although Grandma had passed a week ago, her body seemed as if she could still wake up again, though highly unlikely. The thread of denial snapped as the funeral attendant lowered the blinds to the crematorium. My mother had departed. This was final. I put my hands together in prayer, bowed my head, and said a silent goodbye and thank you.

*****

Many people had passed on in my lifetime. I'd been to many funerals, but only two cremations, and both in Japan—my mother's parents. Every culture has their own rituals to honor the dead, and I had experienced this custom for my grandparents in Japan, so I thought it was "normal." After a family member passed, the body was then returned to their place of primary dwelling, where it rested in the living room for people to come to express condolences and view the departed. The cremation was just for immediate family, and the process included examining the ashes. We were given very long chopsticks and carefully placed the ashes into the urn. I wasn't as close to my grandparents as I was with my mother and was grateful I wouldn't need to do that for her. A sense of peace came over me when I saw their ashes, a serenity that everything had turned to ash. It was final. Life that once was on this earth no longer existed. Receiving the urn symbolized completion, although the process up to this moment had been difficult.

I didn't want to put myself through the sorting of her ashes in such a delicate emotional state. With my grandparent's deaths, I was able to more fully accept the reality, and the tears, although they never stopped completely, were more drops of remembrance rather than streams of pain and loss. I wondered if my grieving process would be longer with my mother without this opportunity to examine her ashes.

As the days rolled over and I neared the two-week mark after quarantine, I felt more ready to leave my mother's house. I had soaked in enough of her energy to take home with me, and although there were never enough walks to take through Kings Park, I knew I could return again. But nothing would ever be the same. Not after COVID. Not after the loss of my mother.

As much as I wanted to stay and help finish up cleaning my mother's house completely, I needed to get back to my family and life in New York. I did as much as I could and had to leave the rest for my sisters. I prepared eight meals to carry back with me, just in case I had an unexpected delay somewhere.

By the time I left, I had started eating some chicken and beef and was getting back to the same diet I had been on when I arrived in Perth. Also, outside of my bitchen and cooking in my mother's actual kitchen, I had upgraded from slow-boiled vegetables to much tastier stir-fries.

My health was still touch-and-go, but the symptoms associated as precursors for seizures were at bay and although my heart rate was often high, it wasn't as high for as long. I worried less about having a heart attack.

HOME

Upon returning home, I was fully prepared to do a ten-day, at-home quarantine as the CDC website indicated I'd need to. I received a call from contact tracing an hour after I walked into my house asking me if I had any COVID-related symptoms. Of course, I still had a runny nose—it was spring and in the full bloom of allergy season—but I denied it. I was released immediately from quarantine. I was utterly confused.

Do I need a COVID test? Nope.

Can I go back to work? Yes.

Are you sure? I work in health care. Yes.

This completely contradicted everything I had read online, as well as the handout I had received on the plane. I asked contact tracing to email me an official discharge from quarantine, which they did immediately. I didn't tell anyone at work that I had been discharged from quarantine. I decided to quarantine anyway.

Being home with my kids and fur babies and in my familiar environment was medicine to my soul. I was immediately soothed with hugs. It was great to reconnect with everyone, and a sense of normalcy took hold. I was on a little "high" at first, relieved that I had made it back without any additional drama. The only minor hiccup was at the Perth airport. As an Australian citizen, I had to apply for an exemption to leave the country, which was misleading as my primary residence was in the United States. I was held up while the airline called the U.S. consulate to confirm I wasn't an escapee.

I was probably running on fumes and adrenaline for the first week or so, but then I was hit with severe exhaustion and emotional turbulence. It was like riding a rollercoaster in the dark, not knowing what twist or upside turn was coming next. There were days when I took two naps and I could still barely function. There were moments when I felt OK, then hit a wall of fatigue and was out cold within seconds. These collapse episodes were completely unpredictable; it was like a storm that wasn't on the forecast, and I was not prepared to deal with it. My emotions were on the surface and tears were a hair-trigger away. I learned to cope by not leaving my house, although I was worried I would become a total recluse. My friends reached out to connect, but there were times, as ridiculous as this may sound when my phone felt too heavy to hold. As a result, I often went days without responding to my friends. This caused some panicked responses since I typically answered before they put their phones down. I retreated into another box. It just seemed like too much energy to engage with anyone outside of work. I put up a wall and hid away from plain sight.

I allowed myself to rest as much as I needed. When I was

ready to reintroduce exercise, I did so gradually. The first month, other than a little stretching, I didn't move a whole lot. I allowed my instincts to guide me through this process and gauge how much energy I had at the moment to decide what I could tolerate. When I got very sick after being exposed to the toxic mold that caused my mast cell disease in the first place, I spent the first year mostly bedridden, on average in bed up to eighteen hours a day. I was so weak that walking to the bathroom was strenuous. This time I was nowhere close to that level of fatigue, but I had a barometer to gauge by. Again, I went through a process of rebuilding strength and stamina—a road well traveled.

I felt stronger as the days passed and turned into weeks. I even managed to get out of the house, not just to get the mail, but to take walks around the block at first, then longer walks in my neighborhood, and eventually out into the park.

I knew my physical body would heal with time. As for the rest of me, I was less confident. I knew this re-integration would be more emotional, a healing that would be less linear than in the physical body. Steering through this arena, as well as managing the fear of the unknown, tended to magnify the intensity. My default setting was to do everything very quickly, and though I wanted to bolt through the unknown territory stealthily, my approach turned out to be like riding a unicycle across an unfinished highway that was marbled with cobblestones and large boulders, blindfolded on crack. After a few scraped knees, head bumps, and a bruised ego, I conceded to go back to the drawing board about my approach to healing. Basically, I was lost and had no idea which way to go or what to do.

Hoping to still wing it without any structured game plan, I found solace in my four-legged friends. I hadn't wanted to talk about my inner world too much, as it felt too raw, and I feared talking about it too early would expose my wounds to harsh elements. One half-wit told me that I just needed to forget about my mother and move on with my life. I wasn't feeling strong enough to duke out this type of conversation with anyone else. Also, the sheer energy that it took to converse wasn't energy I had to spare in the early weeks of my return. But my little fur babies embodied unconditional love and allowed me to have mini-therapy sessions. I asked my cats and dogs, "Do you miss Grandma? I bet you do. I do too." And, "Will I ever stop missing Grandma? I hope it won't be this bad tomorrow." My little cats looked at me with wide eyes and nuzzled against my arms while my dogs licked my face after eating cat poop.

There were days I cried more often than my eyes were dry. I missed my parents more than I could have ever imagined and the sadness felt like it engulfed my spirit. I felt paralyzed by my loss. I just let myself be and without being too self-indulgent and getting totally lost, I permitted myself to meander through my thoughts and feelings, and explored whatever presented from the depths of my being. I was still mostly inside my own prism, not ready to emerge back into society.

One of my friends asked, "Why don't you talk to a therapist, like a real therapist, the two-legged type?"

And I responded, "Because there is nothing that they will be able to say or do that will change the situation." It wasn't that I had issues with my grief. It seemed appropriate for what I had experienced. I didn't think it was necessary for me at that time. Slowly, over time, I noticed that sometimes there was a day that I didn't cry at all. I was careful not to label that as a better day than the days that I cried all day.

After a couple of months passed, I started to see friends with some regularity. The general feedback was that I didn't look terrible. I didn't have enough curiosity at the time to ask them what they had been anticipating seeing. Did they expect me to meet them with an axe wedged in my skull?

I touched base with friends who had lost both parents and asked them if this feeling of emptiness ever went away, and to my dismay, it hadn't gone away for many. If anything, the void had broadened. They did encourage me with the idea that many learned to "manage" this void and this space that had been created. It could be an opportunity to invite different things into my life. And even though my parents weren't here on a physical level, I could connect with them in unique ways. They might even choose to communicate with me. And with a little time, after the dust settled, I would be able to connect with them. I found them in music, in nature, while driving the car, walking the dogs, and sometimes they'd even drop in while I was sitting on the toilet.

Despite feeling physically stronger and crying less frequently, my mind was slower to heal. I started to see a pattern where I was so distracted that I lost the ability to finish sentences. I found that I would start a sentence with some level of cognition, but by mid-sentence, the thought had been lost, and I had taken a radical turn into a mine field, detonating bombs and taking cover from my own unwitting emotional shards. My close friends gently told me I needed professional help after listening to nonlinear conversations: "I went grocery shopping to buy zucchini to make veggie lasagna…and that's why I'll never get over the loss of my mother."

I had only briefly experienced the denial of my mother's passing before she died, but I didn't realize that could also be expanded to encompass the denial over how much her loss had impacted my well-being and ability to function. The first four people who had kindly told me that I looked like I was struggling and needed help, I disregarded. But after the fifth person told me that my emotional spillage was so large that it took over an entire conversation, with worldwide domination-style force, I started to get the hint that I was out of control.

As things have usually gone in my life, when I pay no heed to more subtle messages from my subconscious mind, the cry for help tends to get louder and more obvious until I get the point. It often starts as a whisper and slowly increases to a megaphone spitting in my face with red siren lights. The particular day when I got the final message, the warning sign itself unhinged and hit me over the head. I had already been having a rough day as my mother's birthday was approaching, and usually, around this time, I could have traveled to see her. I was aware that I was deeply immersed in my feelings of missing her, but I decided I couldn't do anything about it. Feeling lonely as my kids were at camp and having taken some time off from work to recuperate, it was a perfect storm for Pandora's box to open and catapult out what had been locked up.

I thought it might be a healthy distraction to go on a date and try to get back some sense of normalcy. We had met earlier that year, but due to my trip and other circumstances, there had been a large gap between dates. I had intended to make it a fun date, to keep it light and to avoid talking about my mother at all costs.

Things went well, and it seemed like there was a genuine connection and mutual interest. The conversation turned when we started to talk about when we would see each other again.

Coincidentally, my date's father's birthday was just two days before my mother's, and he mentioned that his family had organized a weekend-long celebration for him, so he would be tied up over the weekend. It was obviously unintentional, but this reminded me it was my mother's birthday in a few days, and this was the beginning of the end. It was the straw that broke the camel's back and pushed me over my limits. He looked at me with care, noticed there was something wrong, and asked if I was OK. "It's my mother's birthday too this week."

"I'm sorry, Momo, that you won't be able to spend it with her." And just those words were enough for me to finally crack. A flood of intense grief came up to the surface. "Mo, are you OK? You look so sad and teary eyed." I just couldn't allow myself to have an emotional apocalypse, I feared I was going to look insane, so I took all my energy and shut all my systems down. I went into a dozen boxes. And although I was able to shut down the grief, I lost the ability to have any level of conversation with the amount of energy it took to control my emotions.

I tried to speak, but only gibberish came out of my mouth. Occasionally I composed a three-word sentence with great effort, "I go pee," but the majority of what came out were half words, mutterings, and grunts. "Thi... bla... hin..." I was mortified as I couldn't have timed this better, embarrassed beyond words that this was the first guy that I had met in a very long time that I really liked. I wanted to seal myself into my box and ship myself off to Antarctica. After a while of total silence on my end and unable to even make eye contact, shaking with my arms wrapped around my knees in the fetal position, he coaxed me gently out of rigor mortis. I finally got a sentence out, "I feel like I just had emotional diarrhea on you, I'm sorry." He told me to stop apologizing, then I said I was sorry for saying I'm sorry. It was time to slap the "I need help" sticker onto my forehead.

Horrified that I had lost all composure, I called up Annie, one of my close friends whom I considered a big sister to me. She had lost both of her parents and I wanted to hear her advice and experience of how she had recovered from it. I leaped straight into my recent romantic disaster and Annie laughed, "Well, at least it wasn't real diarrhea." Which was true, but nonetheless didn't make me feel any better. She told me a story about when she was only a few months into her relationship and she and her boyfriend had planned a romantic Valentine's getaway. On the first day there, she ate something bad and had horrible food poisoning. She woke up in the middle of the night with severe stomach cramps, and while still in bed, she lost total bowel function. She spurted liquid, hot, yellow, smelly shit out of her ass onto her boyfriend. Despite the shit-smearing experience, he didn't leave her, and it's been fourteen years. She reassured me that, in comparison, my metaphorical shit was a lightweight problem, and if a guy couldn't handle that, then he wasn't worth keeping, and I could plunge him out of my life.

After my dysfunctional date, it became apparent that he had

lost interest, and over the next month, followed a gradual withdrawal. It ended with me getting plunged.

I was nowhere in the clear in terms of healing the loss of my mother, and getting dumped amplified the grief. He couldn't articulate his reasons for his waning interest. He used the classic line, "It's me, not you."

I wondered if my mother had thought this, too, when she passed away. "Momo, don't take it personally, it's my timing, it's got nothing to do with you." But it takes time and perspective I didn't have at the moment to see these things. It's possible they both had to leave for reasons unbeknownst to me. Maybe my mother had commitments with the reincarnation committee. And maybe he just hated the shampoo I used. Or better still, his reasons for drifting had nothing to do with me. It's feasible that he went for a walk and lost his penis. More questions I would never get answers to.

I contemplated the parallel dynamic of my childhood where my parents weren't available to take care of even my basic needs during a time of crisis, and again I found myself abandoned by another person I had cared about. The emotionally challenging circumstances I was experiencing exacerbated the blow.

We all attract partners who reflect back the familiarity of our relationships with our parents, and until this energy is brought forward from the unconscious mind to the conscious and the entire biochemical, energetic, and emotional system is rerouted, we will continue to bring the same types of relationships into our lives to play out over and over again. I had unwittingly replayed the same drama. It's not much different than watching the same episode of Days of our Lives over and over again. It's time for me to watch the next episode, or better still, to direct an episode in my own personal drama where I get away with stealing an entire box of cookies from the pantry unnoticed.

I picked up my Humpty Dumpty pieces and tried to figure out how to put myself together again. If all the king's horses and men couldn't put Humpty together again, what chance did I have? I have stopped asking why I've fallen off the wall—I've stopped asking why I even sat on the wall in the first place—because I couldn't figure it out. Yet here I was, in pieces, and I needed to get myself together. If the death of my mother and the time spent in quarantine didn't push me over into a deep depression, I feared that the added sum of all this heartache and trauma would make me break in two. I braced myself for the worst, not knowing how bad it could get. I took it easy and checked in with myself regularly. Was I going to end up homeless from emotional disturbance, running through the streets stark naked, claiming I had superpowers? I talked to my trusted friends. I connected with my therapist, I took care of my body, I ate well, and I tried my best to say kind things to myself.

Rationally speaking, a few dates with someone shouldn't

have pushed me over the edge, but in this case, it was the tipping point. One unfortunate date was the catalyst. Having an awareness was nice and all, but floundering through the giant ball of pain and sadness was another issue.

My solar plexus and heart felt shattered and empty. After treading in murky water, the sediment settled a little and I was finally able to tease apart the loss of the potential relationship from the loss of my mother, as well as so many other things that I had lost but hadn't fully grieved. Suppressed sadness, collectively held inside my torso, was finally cleansed.

Over time, I could perceive what looked like a pretty standard reaction to a breakup and the experience of the wounds of all the grief we have lived reopening. After a few weeks, I patted myself up and down and found I was still all in one piece. I did a happy dance. I was OK.

I acknowledged that whatever work I had done on myself all those years ago had held its integrity. I had cracked a little, but I didn't crumble. It wasn't another Adam situation. I didn't go into the depths of despair that I traveled into in my twenties, war zones I would not wish upon anyone. In terms of breakups, I fared just fine. I passed with a C+, and considering my relationship GPA was 0.2, it was a step up in my view.

I don't think I'll ever be "done" grieving the loss of my

parents. I don't expect that to happen, nor do I want to ever stop missing them. But the loss found a place in my mind and heart that was held with tenderness rather than a constant pain that was probing relentlessly with jagged edges. And maybe this was just serendipity, but as I went through the loss of the potential romantic relationship, it somehow positively affected the grief process for my mother too. I got a two-for-one deal. I have heard that hell is often a shortcut to heaven. At least I got an extra push to catapult out of darkness and was heading somewhere different, hopefully, better than where I had been. Almost grateful that I had been dumped, as it seemed like it had accelerated my healing process with my mother, I got off the stretcher, removed my bandages, and slipped on a pair of ballet shoes. I was ready to start dancing again.

There is a beautiful Japanese art form called Kintsugi, where broken pottery pieces are glued together with gold. As perfect as a piece of new pottery without any cracks is, how much more interesting and unique is a broken piece of pottery with the artistry of golden paint? Much like this, I hoped that the way my soul broke into pieces over and over again through disappointment and hardship, the golden threads that sewed me together in an intricate manner, told a more layered, intriguing story of my life. Maybe the mending of my soul is just the alchemical process wherein the clay that breaks over and over again and is slowly put back together with gold, in the end, turns completely into gold. So just maybe every time I break a little, I can dare to say that I will no longer see myself as shattered or imperfect but a step closer to becoming pure gold.

At the natural history museum, one of my favorite standing exhibitions is of a tree that endured a fire and, even after its damage, continued to grow around its wounds. The damaged part remained, unable to regenerate, but around it, the tree continued to grow, creating a unique pattern of life. As it grew, the damaged part looked smaller in comparison to the new, healthy part of the tree, safeguarding the wound.

I hope with time, I can stand tall like this tree, telling the world I may have this wound, but I'll continue to grow anyway. Well, at least until some asshole chops me down and sticks me in a museum.

Life is unfair and trying to make it fair wasn't going to offer me a solution, nor would finding reasons for the traumatic nature of my childhood, the unpleasant quarantine experience, the circumstances of my mother's death, my health challenges, or all of my breakups combined.

Healing didn't miraculously happen with an "aha" moment when I worked out the roots of human anguish; it happened when I allowed myself to experience my feelings fully on all levels—physical, emotional, and energetic—and processed and released the loss, pain, and suffering.

I learned how to charter my life in a way to feel less bogged down by all the psychological debris I had picked up throughout my challenges. In the absence of the suffering was just an emptiness—a void. Now my commitment is to my own personal growth, to watch my self-esteem grow to healthy proportions. I'm going to give this my everything, my 100 percent, and I'm happy to say that I'll fail often and will make the same mistakes over and over again. And this is what I love about myself the most, my acceptance of my humanity. Just like taking a dance class or laughing at how terrible I look, I devour the satisfaction of seeing tiny amounts of progress.

This, in a hypoallergenic nutshell, exemplifies how I view my life as a whole. I delight in these morsels of self-improvement. My positive feedback loop, my dopamine receptors, my pleasure center, and my reward systems are hooked into very small personal achievements.

This is what my mother gave me that has saved me: her pride in every tiny step that I achieved that overran every trauma I encountered. It was this seed that she planted in me when I was a baby, the ability to keep growing like the tree that had encountered the fire.

When the famous cellist Pablo Casals was asked at age ninety-five, two years prior to his passing, why he still practiced every day, he responded, "Because I think I'm making real progress."

This is what I wish to hold onto every day that I too, am making progress. As my mother took me to ballet class, she would say to me, "Look! What you thought you could never do before, you're doing now."

There will be days that I will fail gloriously. There will be days that I will retreat back into my personal quarantine box. And when I am ready, I will eat my way out of the cardboard box, a literal metaphor for my bland diet. I will hatch out of isolation and open up my heart to connect with others who have also hatched, and to have the courage to love again.

ABOUT THE AUTHOR

Momoko Uno lives in Westchester, NY, with her children, six cats, two dogs, and an oversized hamster. In high school, she received a C- for English writing and was told she was too dumb to go to medical school. She was also a poor listener, didn't take advice well, and has, against all odds, maintained a private practice in New York City for over two decades.

Made in the USA
Monee, IL
30 May 2023

34976701R00115